'Finally . . . a book just about Early Phonics! This no-nonsense text provides a wide range of practical ideas to support early phonic development. Whether you're based here in the UK or elsewhere in the world, this is a must-read!'

– **Matthew Klimcke,** Education Consultant

'Rose Blair draws upon her extensive work in Early Years settings and classrooms to draw together the statutory requirements in relation to the early development of literacy and provision that supports the foundations of later, proficient reading. Blair offers accessible theory alongside lessons from classrooms and settings across the country. It is refreshing to see a book give such generous space to practitioner voice, too often neglected in writing on this vitally important topic. Blair makes clear her commitment to inclusivity. She offers a range of practical solutions to the question of how best to meet the needs of diverse cohorts, and – like a sharply enunciated sound – makes crystal clear the critical importance of a rich and empowering foundation of early language development.'

– **Martin Galway,** National Literacy Trust

The Right Start to Phonics

If children are to access all phonics teaching effectively, they first need to know how to tune into and manipulate the sounds specifically needed for reading. *The Right Start to Phonics* shows readers how they can support children in gaining the skills they need to listen with accuracy, to differentiate between, manipulate and understand the sounds we hear. This experience will give them the knowledge and understanding needed to hear letter sounds and blend them together to eventually read words.

Drawing on the latest research, the book shows how Early Phonics can be embedded across your provision and fit into the daily routine of any setting or school. Part One explores the role of play, the adult and the learning environment in supporting early phonics and listening skills. This is followed by a wealth of easy-to-use activities to support the development and refinement of these hugely important skills in our youngest children. All the activities are simple to implement with easily sourced resources and cover a range of early phonic skills.

Full of playful, active and fun ideas to help young children develop the auditory skills they need to access the phonic code, this is essential reading for all early years and primary educators and parents.

Rose Blair has been an Early Years teacher for almost four decades, spending most of the past decade as an EY adviser for one of England's leading national school improvement providers. She founded *The Right Start EY Consultancy* based in North Yorkshire, supporting all areas of the EYFS, with expertise in early literacy.

If you would like more information or want to get in touch, please see Rose Blair's consultancy website www.therightstartearlyyears.co.uk.

The Right Start to Phonics

A Guide to Supporting Excellence in Early Phonics

Rose Blair

Routledge
Taylor & Francis Group

LONDON AND NEW YORK

Designed cover image: © Ekaterina Demidova / Getty Images

First edition published 2025
by Routledge
4 Park Square, Milton Park, Abingdon, Oxon, OX14 4RN

and by Routledge
605 Third Avenue, New York, NY 10158

Routledge is an imprint of the Taylor & Francis Group, an informa business

British Library Cataloguing-in-Publication Data
A catalogue record for this book is available from the British Library

ISBN: 978-1-032-58691-5 (hbk)
ISBN: 978-1-032-58690-8 (pbk)
ISBN: 978-1-003-45108-2 (ebk)

DOI: 10.4324/9781003451082

Typeset in Bembo
by Apex CoVantage, LLC

For Jordan and Sam, who keep me grounded with their sense, knowledge and laughter. Thank you.

Contents

Acknowledgements

To Katie Callaghan, for your professional wisdom, knowledge and inspiration. You have provided me with endless positivity and encouragement. But also for your input with ideas, activities, advice and diligence. Thank you.

To Charlotte A, Charlotte B, Lisa, Donna and Julie for your time and expertise that you willingly shared. Thank you.

To Nick, Shannon and Albie, Lisa, Lydia and Eva, thank you for your incredible patience, understanding and sense of fun.

To Luke Whitaker and Helen Grundy grateful thanks for your youthful knowledge and kind support!

To Lynn, thank you for your creative ideas, especially for our youngest children.

And to Chris Moore, for endlessly being my 'port in a storm', for your wisdom, your time, diligence and your patience. Thank you.

'The Sound Collector' from Pillow Talk by Roger McGough reprinted by permission of Peters Fraser & Dunlop (www.petersfraserdunlop.com) on behalf of Roger McGough, CBE.

Part One

Introduction

In this chapter

In the Introduction, I will explain the principles of 'Early Phonics' and why the embedding of Early Phonic skills is a vital first component for young children on their journey towards becoming competent and confident readers. Phonics teaching is briefly examined to contextualise the importance of creating strong foundations in Early Phonics. The book is aimed at all adults who are invested in encouraging early reading skills, so ideas are shared about how the book will offer information and support to parents, teachers and practitioners.

What is meant by Early Phonics?

I have quite deliberately entitled this book *The Right Start to Phonics* although it is not exactly 'Phonics' as such that I will be exploring. The focus of the book is what I have called 'Early Phonics'.

Early Phonics is about listening to and hearing sounds around us, discriminating between these sounds and understanding that we can make and change sounds in many different ways, and it's about hearing sounds in stories, rhymes, poems and songs.

Robust learning in Early Phonics will ensure that when children begin their own individual phonics journey, they will be able to make rapid progress because the auditory learning that takes place in Early Phonics is embedded and ready to be built upon.

DOI: 10.4324/9781003451082-2

The Right Start to Phonics

This book is in two sections:

> **Part One** explores the guiding principles when introducing children from birth onwards to Early Phonics. It will equip adults with the knowledge and understanding needed to underpin their teaching of Early Phonics across the Early Years Foundation Stage (EYFS) and beyond.
>
> **Part Two** contains a broad range of activities that will support the embedding of these principles in a playful way in line with the expectations for teaching and learning across the EYFS.

The activities have been organised into three sections:

■ **Sounds Around** – which involves all of the sounds we may hear in our environments

■ **Sounds We Make** – which is about sounds we create

■ **Sounds With Words** – which includes songs, voice sounds, poems and rhymes

The activities are versatile, using simple resources when required, and are adaptable for use in many settings. They are designed for children of varying ages and a diverse range of learning needs.

Why are Early Phonic skills so vital?

What often seems to be missing from current phonics teaching is a deep focus on the *incredibly important* area of Early Phonics. Early Phonics are the skills that will provide the foundations for all the phonics learning to come. The skills are based on auditory discrimination: the ability to hear, focus their listening and differentiate between, manipulate and understand sounds we hear. This fine-tuned knowledge and understanding of sound will prepare children to hear and use the phonic code when they are taught this in Systematic Synthetic Phonics (SSP) sessions taught from the age of 5 in English schools. This later SSP stage is where children are taught a sound linked to a letter shape and then are required to blend these together to read words. Children are taught this stage of phonics from September when they enter school in the Reception year.

A strong foundation in Early Phonics is needed to ensure every child is ready and prepared to access this later phonic learning; learning which will enable them to read and write effectively.

The phonic sounds are taught from each child's first days in school, so you can see how challenging this will be for a child whose grounding in Early Phonics is not already established. How can they be expected to hear, recognise and remember letter sounds and then blend them together to read when they are not able to focus their listening effectively?

Preparing for future phonic learning

Without skills in Early Phonics, everything in our children's future phonic world will be so much harder. Phonics isn't a 'one size fits all' as recognised by many proponents of the approach; however, it can be learnt by most. I often talk to teachers who have children in their class who are struggling to make sense of the phonic approach to reading. My initial advice to them is always . . . try more of the Early Phonics (Phase One in old Letters and Sounds). Don't bombard the children with more of the same phonemic learning that will lead to them becoming demoralised and frustrated as they struggle to recognise letters or match them to sounds and blend them. This is not what they need. They need a different approach. They need to go back to basics.

This principle should certainly not be limited to the EYFS. If children are older and are finding reading a challenge, then it is always worth trying again with the Early Phonics activities. I believe that Early Phonics will help these children reaffirm their reading foundations. We need to close gaps in reading ability and support those who are disadvantaged or vulnerable to underachievement, whose challenges can come in many guises.

Imperative foundations

I want to reiterate the importance of Early Phonics. For many things in life, it's the foundations that need to be as strong as they possibly can be, and Early Phonics are the foundations for cracking and using the phonic code. Once cracked, the whole world becomes so much more of a rich, exciting place – one where children have started to take their first steps on their independent reading journey.

Phonics in a nutshell

Phonics is the preferred method currently used to teach children to read and write in England and in other languages where an alphabet is used. It is a system where each letter (called a *grapheme* in its written form) has a sound allocated to it (the sound being a *phoneme*). In Systematic Synthetic Phonics (SSP), which is the system used in England, the letter sounds are *blended* in order, from left to right, to read words. For example, 'c/a/t' spoken softly from left to right, when blended effectively, will make the word 'cat'. It is important that the sounds are voiced softly in order that no additional sounds are created e.g. if a hard 'm' was uttered, then the actual sound might be 'm-uh' (this extra 'uh' is called 'adding a schwa') thus adding two extra phonemes to a word such as 'mum' as it would become 'm-uh/u/m-uh!

The putting together of sounds to read words is called *blending,* and the breaking down of words in order to spell them is called *segmenting*.

The entire alphabetic system is broken into phonemes that include some 'digraphs' – two letters together as with 'ch' or 'sh' and some are 'trigraphs', which might be 'igh', for example. There are other nuances to this system that children are required to learn, but for now, I will limit this to one important exception to the phonic code. These are what might be referred to as 'tricky words' or 'common exception words', which are words that cannot easily be sounded out. In the early stages of phonics, words such as 'go' or 'the' are termed 'tricky words'. The reading of these words is approached slightly differently, not necessarily just using the SSP system of blending.

In addition to this, there are two terms that will appear throughout the book. Phonological awareness and Phonemic awareness. To clarify, I am calling Phonological awareness the skill of being aware of sound, hearing sounds, playing with and manipulating sounds. Phonemic awareness is part of Phonological awareness but is much more specifically about letter sounds (phonemes) and how these are used to enable reading and writing.

An epiphany

I was browsing in a bookshop one Saturday afternoon, and I happened upon a teaching aid that sparked something within me. I had heard of phonics. My age meant that I hadn't been taught phonics myself in school. I was instantly engrossed. I thought of nothing else all weekend, devoured the contents of the teaching aid, and went into school on Monday to ask the Head Teacher if she would mind me trialling this concept. I was fortunate that she was both progressive in her thinking and trusted me. She had clearly heard of reading being taught through the phonic approach and was happy for me to give it a go. And it worked. Within our school, a large infant school, 23 different languages were spoken by the children. In my Reception class, I had a broad range of abilities and a fair proportion of children whose first language was not English, but we flew! The children made sense of the sounds I was teaching them and adored the fun actions that arose from brief stories linked to the sounds. These actions then supported the children in remembering each sound and helped them make swift connections to the shapes of the letters. It all fitted together very nicely. We learned the 'tricky words' and obviously still maintained the rich reading and literacy environment that we had always had. Only now, the children had a grasp of the 'nuts and bolts' that were holding all of that reading curriculum together.

Nuts and bolts

This is how I've come to see phonics: the 'nuts and bolts' of reading and the fundamental skills that effective reading for life is built upon. However, if a child's 'nuts and bolts' aren't tightening with the same twist over and over, it's time to try a different-sized nut! Go back to the beginning and have some more fun by undertaking more Early Phonics activities. Once the children are developmentally ready and are readily tuning into sounds, understanding sounds, what they are and how to use them, they will hear and use the phonic code effectively.

Environmental sounds

Sound is an inevitable feature of our lives. Even as we sit in our homes in apparent silence, we can find ourselves bombarded with sounds, perhaps from our central heating systems, household appliances and family members, to sounds from outside, such as aircraft and other transport passing by, birds and people going about their daily business. It all mounts up to a continuous accompaniment to our existence.

As adults, we are usually able to block out this peripheral noise, tuning out those sounds that are not needed on a daily basis for any purpose. That is definitely an essential skill for us, but before we as humans have learnt to do that, before we develop that ability, it is essential that we learn to *tune in* to sounds first.

Learning to discriminate between these sounds

We then need to recognise and categorise each of these sounds. I'm certain that this must be part of our fight or flight response, where we essentially need to know which sounds are to be recognised as a threat. This is clearly happening with our children from birth and even before! They are beginning to discriminate between some sounds – the familiar voice of a parent or sibling perhaps. Moving forward, they will need to learn how to use these sounds, eventually for speaking and to keep themselves safe, then for reading and writing. This is where our work starts as enabling adults who can already speak, read and write and have the desire to impart this knowledge to the next generation.

An interesting moment . . .

Recently, when flicking through radio stations, I came upon an item discussing The Sound Collector, a poem by the poet Roger McGough. It punctuated my thinking. It was interesting because two girls who were discussing his poem with the radio presenter had clearly put their own interpretation into it, which is just what I'd expect any poem to incite: an individual response. We all have our own interpretations of anything creative. But when Roger McGough explained what his thoughts on the poem were about, this is where it really resonated with me because it aligned so profoundly with my thinking about Early Phonics. I'll share the poem with you:

A stranger called this morning
Dressed all in *black* and grey
Put *every* sound into a bag
And *carried* them away

The *whistling* of the kettle
The *turning* of the lock
The *purring* of the kitten
The *ticking* of the clock

The *popping* of the toaster
The *crunching* of the flakes
When you *spread* the marmalade
The *scraping* noise it makes

The *hissing* of the *frying* pan
The *ticking* of the grill
The *bubbling* of the bathtub
As it *starts* to fill

The *drumming* of the raindrops
On the windowpane
When you do the washing-up
The *gurgle* of the drain

The *crying* of the baby
The *squeaking* of the chair
The *swishing* of the curtain
The *creaking* of the stair

A *stranger* called this morning
He didn't *leave* his name
Left us only silence
Life will *never* be the same

'The Sound Collector' from *Pillow Talk* by Roger McGough reprinted by permission of Peters Fraser & Dunlop (www.petersfraserdunlop.com) on behalf of Roger McGough, CBE

Roger McGough explained that he had been thinking about the peripheral sounds that we all hear, all of the time, the continuous, percussive theme tune to our daily lives.

We need to consider that our children have an abundance of sounds to discriminate between. Their challenge comes as they are confronted with having to filter their way through them. With the ever-increasing plethora of electronic devices we now have at our fingertips, children have far more sounds now than we, as adults, had to contend with when we were children.

All of these noises are constant in all of our lives, so with the poem in mind, it highlighted to me the cacophony to which our children are constantly being exposed.

The importance of hearing sounds

What this means for us as educators is that we need to teach our children effectively how to discriminate between and filter the sounds that are being heard. This will enable them to isolate individual sounds effectively.

Once children can do this, they will be able to do the same with phonemes when they are introduced to the phonic code.

If children can hear and learn to manipulate sounds really effectively, it will make their journey into the phonic code so much simpler, enabling them to blend and segment individual phonemes to read and write skilfully and understand and implement the phonic code with ease.

The Right Start to Phonics and the Statutory Framework

The information shared in the first part of the book, the guidance section, strongly reflects the 'guiding principles' of the EYFS Statutory Framework (DfE 2023). The elements of the unique child, positive relationships and enabling environments with supportive adults are all included, and the guidance reiterates the importance and impact of learning and development.

Part two of the book, the activities, again reflects these elements but with the addition of a deep understanding of the need for learning with young children to be playful and active for it to be meaningful. *The Right Start to Phonics* will robustly support learning in Communication and Language. This is the area of learning in the Statutory Framework that encourages the development of spoken language, conversation, reading and sharing stories and rhymes and it underpins all other areas of learning.

Literacy, as an area of learning, is also well-supported throughout the book. Early Phonics embraces elements of both language comprehension and word reading, preparing children well for their future phonic learning. Other areas of learning in the EYFS are also supported, although in less depth. The activities encompass elements of maths, understanding the world, social development and music, for example, through play.

Teaching reading in the EYFS

I fundamentally support the teaching of phonics as one of the starting points for teaching reading, but there are other facets to learning to read that are equally important. Children need a rich reading diet – a smorgasbord of written language that includes a word-rich learning environment. They need to see contextualised print that has a purpose. We should be exposing children to print in many places, drawing their attention to letters and words, books, poetry, magazines and print in their locality that they are familiar with, and they should see adults modelling reading so they understand it is something both necessary and enjoyable. These things would all add to the rich reading diet that children need.

There are some concerns I have about phonics teaching. I am concerned that, in many cases, the requirement for teaching phonics is too prescriptive and 'stationary'. The teaching is often receptive rather than interactive and playful. Often, the requirements are not from those who are actually delivering the teaching i.e. those who know their cohorts, know their children and have a deep child-centred understanding that the best way to teach children is through activity and play. This style of static teaching goes against the well-researched practice that has mostly become established across the EYFS in England. Learning is best when there is some intrinsic motivation, and I believe this, for young children, comes through play and playful teaching.

Play needs to underpin Early Phonics

What needs to be at the forefront of any practitioner's mind as they plan to teach Early Phonics (and also later phonics sessions) is a focus on how children learn. In Birth to 5 matters, one of the non-statutory guidance documents for the EYFS, we are reminded that what we provide for children should 'include playful, multisensory and creative experiences and games that promote children's interest in reading and in developing phonics skills and knowledge' (Early Years Coalition 2021:90). This premise is fundamental to the activities included in this book. Early Phonics teaching, therefore, must be playful and fun, not static.

Theorists from Piaget to Vygotsky and Bruner all talk about the importance of play and activity to promote learning. In the context of the EYFS in our Statutory Framework, we are assured that young children need to be active and physically engaging in their learning.

In addition to this, it is important to remember that the age of the child should not dictate the way they are required to learn. We are accustomed in the EYFS to treating each child as unique, and this includes the way they learn. Certainly, if a child of any age is struggling to access the phonic code, what they need is the playful learning of Early Phonics, not only to bolster their confidence but also to ensure they have these early skills embedded.

Who is this book for?

This book is intended to support the broad spectrum of adults working with and spending time with small children. Your experience might be extensive from years working in the sector, or you may be new to the EYFS or even a new parent. Whatever your starting point, there will be information and guidance to support you. It explores how children must be taught to read using the phonic approach and how this is documented in the EYFS guidance. The importance of the learning environment is examined, and the role of the adult in this component of the EYFS is discussed.

Different children, or cohorts of children, will need their learning needs approached in a way that is suited to them. Children will learn skills at different rates and at different times, so as adults, we need to be tuned into this learning and provide the focused skill development needed. The guidance and activities will afford you the opportunity to understand and ultimately create bespoke, fine-tuned learning situations for all children in your care.

Those with experience in the sector

For experienced practitioners, this book will contain some reminders. You might skim through the chapters to find the activities which will invigorate your practice in Early Phonics. The impact of this will be that the children you are working with are extremely well-prepared, in their own time and at their own individual pace, for cracking and effectively using the phonic code.

Those new to understanding learning in the EYFS

It may be that you are studying to become an Early Years educator in some form: a play worker, a teaching assistant, a parent or another relative, or you might be working towards a qualification, perhaps an Early Years practitioner or a trainee teacher. Maybe you have decided to home-school your children or simply just add to their learning journey. The information in this book is both useful and accessible and will give you the confidence not only to teach Early Phonic skills but also to explain why they are such a vital component of a child's reading journey.

Support to focus your thinking and understanding

Part One

At the end of each chapter, you will find **'Points to Peruse and Ponder'**. These all pertain to the chapter that has been read and are intended to help your reflective process. They might be useful to spur some further research you might be interested in, initiate change in your current practice, or they could be used as questions for a team or staff meeting to prompt discussions about your practice. I hope you find them useful.

Part Two

With each of the activities, there are two elements: 'Why?' and 'Making other connections'. These are intended to focus the thinking of the adult.

'Why?' gives the reason for the activity and the skills being developed. I believe that if we understand why we are teaching a skill clearly, then our focused support will be richer.

'Making other connections' illuminates the cross-curricular nature of the activity and the splendidly heterogeneous nature of teaching and learning in the EYFS

Points to peruse and ponder . . .

■ Have you ever considered how you were taught to read? What do you remember about this process?

■ Take a moment to really listen to the sounds around you and become aware of the 'filtering' you are naturally doing each and every day. Consider how this is for small children.

■ Start to consider how you currently approach the teaching of early reading and begin to think about adaptations you might like to make to this process.

References

DfE. 2023. *Statutory Framework for the Early Years Foundation Stage*. London: DfE.

Early Years Coalition. 2021. *Birth to 5 Matters, Reading, Enabling Environments*. St Albans: Early Education.

1 Early Phonics and the Early Years Foundation Stage

In this chapter

This chapter takes a brief look at the current EYFS documentation, both statutory and non-statutory, and how this impacts Early Phonics. Additionally, it reflects upon:

- The nature of learning for young children and how skills will develop for each unique child

- The Characteristics of Effective Learning and how they can support Early Phonics

- Two important elements: how Early Phonics must be an ongoing process and the inclusivity of the activities included in *The Right Start to Phonics*

Teaching requirements in the EYFS

In England, The Statutory Framework for the Early Years Foundation Stage (DfE 2023) lays out all the elements that must frame what our youngest children learn. The document endeavours to ensure that everyone understands the expectations for learning and development. These elements for teaching and learning (the 'educational programmes') are divided into three Prime and four Specific areas.

Clearly, the area of Literacy has the most direct connection to the skills I am sharing in this book, and the teaching of phonics is a requirement for all children. The word 'phonics' itself is somewhat elusive within the document; however, it does say that:

> Skilled word reading, taught later, involves both the speedy working out of the pronunciation of unfamiliar printed words (decoding) and the speedy recognition of familiar printed words.
>
> (DfE 2023)

DOI: 10.4324/9781003451082-3

Early Learning Goals

In a nutshell, the earlier quote describes phonics. Further in the document, there are Early Learning Goals that are a benchmark for what a child might achieve by the end of the Early Years Foundation Stage (EYFS). They indicate that by the end of the Reception year, the children should be able to:

- 'Say a sound for each letter in the alphabet and at least 10 digraphs

- Read words consistent with their phonic knowledge by sound-blending

- Read aloud simple sentences and books that are consistent with their phonic knowledge, including some common exception words' (p. 14)

It is clear that a child would most certainly have had to be taught the phonic code quite specifically to be able to achieve these 'goals'.

Learning new skills

All learning in the EYFS (and in life in general) is intertwined, and as such, Early Phonic skills thread through all the 'educational programmes'. Life isn't compartmentalised; everything we do utilises so many skills, a vast breadth of knowledge and understanding. We employ these skills naturally, instinctively without thinking because we have learnt each skill, probably individually, and then understand how each can be used and combined with others. This is embedded into our psyche.

One of our executive functions is known as 'Working Memory'; this is what I am describing. Working memory is the ability to hold things in our minds and then use them later to make sense of new learning. Some analogies I always think of for this intertwining of skills is when we, as adults, consider the complexities of learning to drive a car, play a musical instrument or maybe learn a sport. All these complex functions might involve some reading, some listening, some maths, some physical skills and some general knowledge. But we need all of these skills combined to move forward to make progress.

In this way, our youngest children's learning, particularly the embedding of taught skills, will be heightened if they are contextualised in this intertwined way. Early Phonics is no different from any other skill.

To ensure that children can access the 'skilled word reading' (as described in the Statutory Framework) with confidence and competence, it is imperative that the learning of Early Phonics' is embedded and takes place consistently, becoming a natural part of each child's early learning. Tuning into all sounds effectively will aid the fine-tuning required for accessing the phonic code. My endeavour is for adults spending time with young children – whether in a home, school or another setting – to be cognisant of this through the information in this book and the accompanying activities.

Non-statutory documentation

There are also two additional 'non-statutory' documents that expand on the 'educational programmes'. They offer further ideas and information about how we can develop children's readiness for reading. The documents are 'Birth to 5 Matters', which describes itself as 'Guidance by the sector for the sector' (Early Education 2021), and 'Development Matters' (DfE 2021), which was commissioned by the DFE and similarly offers support to explain what anyone working or supporting in the EYFS can do to help children learn and develop effectively. If we look at 'Birth to 5 Matters' first, the initial focus on play fits perfectly with the ethos of *The Right Start to Phonics*. Children are going to learn best through play, a theory which has been well-researched and is even supported by the United Nations Convention on the Rights of a Child (1989).

To ensure our approach to teaching Early Phonics is based on sound Early Years theory, it is important for us to recognise that, from theorists as early as Froebel (1782–1852), great value has been placed on play. Freidrich Froebel 'had firm views on play and its place in child development, believing that it fostered enjoyment, emotional well-being and was a fundamental source of benefit' (Pound 2005:15). Play is a natural disposition for children. It gives them the opportunity to explore their world with independence, trying things out, making decisions, making choices and engaging with others if they wish.

'Tuning into' the phonic code

As I have explained, we need children to 'tune into' sounds to enable them to learn what sounds are. To learn and use phonics effectively and efficiently, children will need to pick up on the sounds (phonemes) that match the letter shapes (graphemes) that they are being taught. They then need to manipulate them, blend them together and synthesise them into words that fit the language they are learning.

High-quality learning

This 'tuning into sound' is the element that comes *before* children can access phonics from the age of 5 onwards. I am focusing now on the earliest skills that children will need to embed to enable them to access all future phonic learning effectively.

This learning is going to have a greater impact on the child and become more meaningful if it is approached through a broad range of playful activities. Through the activities in this book, the Early Phonic skills will be introduced to the children by adults and then left for the child or children to revisit independently to embed that learning by exploring and investigating in their own time and in their own way. This is a recognised and proven method of ensuring high-quality learning takes place and is intertwined with existing knowledge, making it meaningful for the child across the EYFS.

Contextualising learning

'Children build on their experiences; therefore, the wider and deeper their exposure, the greater potential they have for secure development. Children need opportunities to practise what they know, to consolidate and apply learning from one context to another, to develop learning from one context to another and to develop new knowledge and skills. Children will build on experiences in the natural, built and virtual worlds' (Early Years Coalition 2021:19). This perfectly illustrates what I was saying about the need to contextualise learning within the framework of the children's individual interests.

Early Phonics should be approached in the same way as other skills taught in the EYFS to ensure the learning has depth and the child gains mastery of the new knowledge.

Early Phonics experienced uniquely

Something else that is fundamental as a principle of the EYFS is that each child is a unique individual. I doubt anyone would want to think otherwise. We all have different facets to our personalities. Children will have different interests and fascinations, and different things might entice them into their learning, but the connection between them all will keep their learning playful and active to maintain and sustain their attention and focus.

Knowing your children

Children will also have had different lifetime experiences. Therefore, the single most important thing you can do as an adult is get to know the children. Understand what makes them tick. What do they like and not like, what provokes reactions in them and what provokes a learning response? Do they prefer lively, social interactions with others, or do they have a quieter nature? Do they respond better to learning indoors or outside? And, of course, understand why this might be. What have been their previous life experiences?

This all needs to be taken into account and responded to. Then, you need to provide appropriate, fine-tuned learning opportunities as a competent adult. In 'Birth to 5 Matters', it explains that 'Children are innately driven to become more competent, and they find and embrace the next stages in their development and learning, meeting challenges and practising to develop their skills and independence' (Early Years Coalition 2021:19).

I would add here that this will only take place readily if the conditions – including the learning environment and adult support – are right, then the children will be in the best place to take that learning forward. In *The Right Start to Phonics*, there are a plethora of ideas for your learning environments as well as a broad range of Early Phonics activities to support this principle.

Adult child relationships

In simple terms, each adult needs to get to know each child to understand how they can support them best to drop in the playful but meaningful (to the unique, individual child) Early Phonics activities. Establishing warm, nurturing relationships will pay dividends for the child, most certainly, but also for you as the adult. The rewards to you as the person who is supporting the child's learning will be boundless if you take the time to get to really know the child. The activities you choose to use and the time at which you decide to use them will be made better by your knowledge of the unique child. Getting to really understand the activities and what you can offer the child at an opportune moment, is equally as important as your knowing the child in the first place. We must value the importance of high-quality interactions and what they might entail as far as Early Phonics is concerned.

Characteristics of Effective Learning

As part of getting to know the unique child, we cannot overlook the all-important Characteristics of Effective Learning. These are exemplified in both the Statutory and Non-Statutory frameworks and illustrate the methods we all, as human beings, learn. Their main headings are Engagement, Motivation and Thinking. These 'Characteristics' are important support structures for meaningful learning. They describe the ways in which children might be learning, and if the characteristics are not used naturally by the children, they need to be taught to them and their development encouraged by adults. They are explained well in the 'Birth to 5 Matters' document.

Engagement

If you think about something you've learned to do recently, perhaps using a new tool or piece of equipment – an electric drill maybe, a sewing machine or even becoming familiar with a new phone or a programme on a computer – you would have to engage with it, find out about it, explore how it works and learn why each component is important. You would certainly make an association with previous experiences from using a similar piece of equipment in the past and blend this new experience into the framework of an old one to make that connection in your understanding. And you would definitely need to 'have a go' yourself! There wouldn't be much point if you didn't!

Motivation

Then, Motivation: being involved and concentrating – it could be somewhat cata-strophic with some of my suggestions if you didn't! Not giving up, 'if at first you don't succeed, try, try and try again!'. The satisfaction and elation when you are successful, when you become more adept and that learning has been embedded.

Thinking

Then we have the thinking – putting your own ideas into practice, making even more connections with other experiences and working through those new ideas.

This very clearly demonstrates that the Characteristics of Effective Learning are truly utilised for our lifelong learning. Children will need to be provided with opportunities to use all Characteristics of Effective Learning and be encouraged to revisit and reuse them many times during this peak time of learning that takes place between birth and 5 years old.

The areas of learning (or 'educational programmes')

'Birth to 5 Matters' explains more about the areas of learning (the 'educational programmes'). As I have said, I often describe learning as being homogenous, and for that reason, Early Phonics can easily be threaded through these areas of learning rather than becoming another discrete area of learning. In addition to the ideas and explanations that follow, with each Early Phonics activity in this book there is an explanation of the connections that can be made between the different areas of learning. This feature will help all adults understand the intertwined nature of learning in addition to equipping them to ensure children receive a broad and balanced curriculum.

Early Phonics and the areas of learning

The areas of learning are described here in the context of Early Phonics and the beneficial experiences they will provide. Starting with the Prime Areas:

Personal, Social and Emotional development (PSED) area of learning is broken down into the sub-sections of Making Relationships, Sense of Self and Understanding Emotions.

- These sections will all be supported with the social aspect of playing a game with at least one other person
- Relationships can be strengthened through fun activities and shared moments of active learning
- Learning to collaborate to play a game or undertake an activity together perhaps, and it will support self-regulation when having to take turns, needing to wait and, on occasions, somebody else being the winner, of course also enjoying the sensation of being a winner yourself!
- The sense of belonging is heightened through the interaction whilst engaging in an activity with another person/people

Communication and Language (CL) This clearly is one of the strongest threads running through the development of learning about sounds, how to hear them and how to manipulate them. This area of learning is broken down into three sub-sections:

Listening and attention

■ This involves hearing sounds, recognising voices and acknowledging them, then listening with interest to new sounds and stories or songs to be really ready to use all of this knowledge and apply it to the learning of phonic letter sounds when they are ready

A very robust connection there. The next sub-section is:

Understanding

■ The language of the game, such as a preposition 'under', 'behind' or listening to a story without pictures

The final sub-section of this area of learning is:

Speaking

■ Children will begin by mimicking the sounds they hear, and this develops through the early stages of talk. This is clearly a precursor to putting those all-important phonic sounds together, demonstrating an understanding of early auditory awareness

Physical development

Physical development is defined as having two main sub-sections, Moving and Handling and Health and Self Care:

■ **Moving and Handling** will be supported by the activities in this book and from the responses and reactions of very young children sitting and taking part in the games to older children using the props and resources when engaging in the activities

■ **Self Care** might then be supported with the use of body parts being named and identified by the children, then used to make sounds

We come now to the Specific areas of learning, the first two being Literacy and Mathematics:

Literacy quite clearly has phonics embedded within it, as you would expect. In the earlier 'ranges', which focus on children with earlier skills, the focus is very much on children engaging with sounds, both noticing them and making them.

Then, even more crucially for early reading, noting and responding to rhythms in songs and rhymes they hear. This, without a doubt, demonstrates that a child has sharpening auditory skills that they are able to acknowledge physically – in a playful manner!

Activities such as filling in missing words from rhymes are also noted, which is another element of Early Phonics.

By 'Range 5', children should be beginning to develop phonological awareness and phonemic awareness, and describe how these might be demonstrated.

In the section 'Enabling Environments', the authors share some ideas for activities (very much focused on 'Reading', as that is the area we are within) that will support this skill development, but they are not focusing sharply on early phonics.

The activities I describe in *The Right Start to Phonics* will be more explicit in nature and help you to develop more fine-tuned activities to, in turn, fine-tune your child/children's skill development.

Now to **Mathematics.** The approach to teaching maths has been through something of a metamorphosis recently. I would not profess to be a huge mathematician, but I am a musician, and these two areas of learning are definitely intertwined. Music is about patterns; rhythm is about patterns, repeating patterns, counting beats and, of course, when you come to formal notation, that is incredibly mathematical.

So mathematically speaking, Early Phonics is therefore very intertwined with this area of learning.

And musically . . .

The rhythms I have mentioned, where you want children to dance, to move to the rhythm of the words necessitates that 'musical ear' to hear rhythms. There are so many rhymes and songs that have that link to maths: Five Little Speckled Frogs, The Wheels on the Bus, Five Currant Buns . . . the list is almost without end.

Moving to **Understanding the World (UW).** I think, with People and Communities, the first sub-section of UW will naturally bring in the songs and rhymes we all have from our cultures, wherever in the world that might be. Whether small children understand the language being used or not, they will still be absorbing the sounds they are hearing, making connections between the words or utterances that sound the same.

UW then moves to The World, and more links can be made here for children to both notice and play with sounds. For example, in Range 3, it says: 'Is curious and interested to explore new and familiar experiences in nature: grass, mud, puddles, plants, animal life'. In the adjacent section 'Positive relationships', it says how adults should draw children's attention to the world around them, including the 'sounds' that they hear. Being outdoors will be the gift of so many more sounds to enhance listening and auditory discrimination. Lying on the grass on a sunny day, perhaps watching clouds pass by and listening to all the sounds you can hear. This is one of the activities later in the book. Then, playing the game elsewhere, on the beach, on the train, by the river. Transferable skills and a transferable/transportable Early Phonics activity.

Figure 1.1 A photograph of a stream and trees on a summer's day.
Source: Photograph taken by the author

Understanding diverse languages

My connection here to the auditory discrimination of children and UW comes with the importance of celebrating other languages. If you are in a class of children with diverse backgrounds, make the most of this by sharing those languages with all of the children.

The children tune into their home language from their earliest days immersed in that language. Therefore, they will perhaps be more phonologically challenged by sounds that are less familiar to them. For example, the sound (or digraph) 'th' does not appear in the French language, so a child learning that sound in an English-speaking school would find it unfamiliar and perhaps harder to annunciate.

Sharing stories, rhymes, songs and games from a broad range of languages will support auditory discrimination and help children to develop their understanding of sounds.

Here, I am reminded of the wonderfully powerful work of Usha Goswami. In her book *Child Psychology, A very short introduction* (Goswami 2014), she discusses the importance of Infant Directed Speech (IDS).

We apparently speak to infants in a particular way that is very different from other ways we speak. It is rhythmic and 'prosodic', a lilting way of using speech. It seems that with IDS, we exaggerate words in ways that can support children to learn where words begin and end, and even more importantly, children actually love to listen to IDS. It captures their attention, which then, in turn, helps them to tune into the sounds we make.

Goswami explains that 'Experiments have shown that even newborns prefer IDS over adult-directed speech' (Goswami 2014: 41). It's the tones and pitches that the children are tuning into in their own ways, and this tuning in is crucial for small children to support their language development and then their phonological and phonemic awareness.

The links to sound continue through Technology, and in Range 3, they mention 'anticipates repeated sounds' when a technological toy is modelled several times. Perhaps even pressing a button on a sound book. Perhaps providing a keyboard in some way for children to interact with, learning and embedding learning through cause and effect when making sounds. Some piano-type keyboards have all sorts of wonderful sounds that can be made when pressing specific buttons as well as other electronic keyboards.

Finally, we come to **Expressive Arts and Design.**
   The first element here is creating with materials. Range 4 talks about using all sorts of musically creative activities in a multisensory way.

- Such activities can be realised through a range of sound makers, singing or vocalising to music being played, noticing the effect they have on musical instruments, whether homemade or conventional

- Find all sorts of ways of making sounds and changing them. Such a strong musical element provides so much depth to early phonics learning, embedding those crucial auditory skills and knowledge! You will find several activities on this theme
- If you are able to play a musical instrument of any kind, then do so and encourage your children to be as musical as they can be – it's all about embedding that phonological awareness. Even if it's just a descant recorder that you can play, move forward with confidence when tooting out 'Baa Baa Black Sheep' as your children will love your skill and will be completely non-judgemental! If you can strum a guitar, you can make virtually every nursery rhyme or Early Years song fit three chords if you are canny enough! The chords are D, A7 and G. You can go online to look at how these chords are made, but just a little finger manipulation and you're a musician capable of impressing any under-5 with your musicianship
- Each and every time you encourage your child or children to engage with musical instruments (and with that, I include any sound-makers … pots and pans, logs, chair legs whatever you have to hand), you will be engaging in both Early Phonics as well as Maths, UW and Music. Tapping beats, playing longer and shorter sounds, repeating rhythms, which sound lasts longest … they will all encourage real, deep listening and internalising rhythm (great to support early reading – the rhythm of the words) and making comparisons

The end of Early Phonics?

In 'Birth to 5 Matters', they describe the children at the end of the EYFS as 'range 6'. Even though these children might be becoming competent at learning and are starting to use the phonic sounds, they still need to continue with the learning of songs, rhymes and to play all of the games suggested in this book to sustain their understanding of Early Phonics. This will bolster their confidence as they come across more complex digraphs (split and otherwise) and contextualise new words that are harder to decipher when employing the phonic code further into their reading journey.

Therefore, the fun and engaging Early Phonic activities should continue. I have made provision for children who are older when creating the games, and it is very easy to tweak the activities to make them appealing to older children.

As explained previously, all children are unique, and they will learn differently. Phonics will not make sense or be useable as a reading strategy if phonological awareness or auditory discrimination is not embedded. This might not happen for some children until they are beyond the EYFS and could even be working within Key Stage 2 (7–11 years of age) for an abundance of reasons. Rather than continue attempting to progress such children through a phonics scheme, which will be frustrating for all, move to use some of the suggested fun activities to develop that skill of auditory discrimination.

A parallel non-statutory document

'Development Matters' that was first published by the Department for Education (DfE) in March 2017 was commissioned to be updated in 2020 by the DfE and was predominantly the work of Julian Grenier, an HT at a Nursery in North London, England at the time. It was written in collaboration with other professionals from across the sector. It gives an overarching view of the ways in which children might learn, but it is not dogmatic and would never be a replacement for the all-important professional judgement that everyone in the sector values so highly. This document is downloadable from the DfE website as an e-document or is accessible as a book, 'Working with the revised Early Years Foundation Stage: Principles into Practice' (Grenier 2020), which is a 'padded out' version.

I mentioned that learning must happen for each and every child, no matter what their starting point might be. This is a thread that runs robustly through the Principles into Practice book (Grenier 2020). 'The gap begins in the early years and is already evident when children begin school aged 5' (p. 13). A simple statement such as this shouts loudly about the importance of our work with young children, and if the widely discussed 'reading gap' is to be addressed, then Early Phonics clearly has a crucial role to play.

Those children who may be from disadvantaged backgrounds, who have been spoken to less in the home for whatever reason, who have missed having stories shared with them and who have no knowledge of nursery rhymes, singing or poetry are those who will benefit so much from learning to tune into sounds, to support their early reading. We will be giving them a huge 'leg up' if we can fill those gaps for them in whatever setting we are in.

Self-regulation and Early Phonics

Another section in the 'Development Matters' document brings self-regulation and executive function to our attention. Basically, executive function will support self-regulation, and self-regulation is about the child's ability to regulate their feelings and emotions, including being patient, waiting for things and being able to face challenges effectively.

Clearly, regularly playing age-appropriate games with others, especially those involving language, talk, conversation and close interaction, are going to help children with self-regulation in abundance!

Parental support with Early Phonics

Further into the 'Development Matters' document, the partnership between settings and parents is discussed. It states that 'It's important to encourage all parents to chat, play and read with their children'. We hope that this book and the information it contains about early phonics is in itself accessible to interested parents and, most certainly, that the information and activities are shared with parents by teachers and other practitioners.

It is crucial that parents support a child's learning in the home, even more so for those who are vulnerable and at risk of disadvantage. The Early Phonics activities in *The Right Start to Phonics* are a fabulous, simple way for this support to be accessible to all.

The Education Endowment Foundation (2021) has conducted research on the benefits of parental support and stated:

> By designing and delivering effective approaches to support parental engagement, schools and teachers may be able to mitigate some of these causes of educational disadvantage, supporting parents to assist their children's learning or their self-regulation, as well as specific skills, such as reading.

Areas of learning

The document then moves to the seven areas of learning. Communication and Language is again the first area to be shared, and as we know, much of this includes Early Phonics, 'Enjoy singing, music and toys that make sounds, listen and respond to a simple instruction, sing a large repertoire of songs', know many rhymes, be able to talk about familiar books' to name just a few. All of these will support early auditory discrimination, a child focusing in on sounds and language.

The areas of learning are explained and there are elements in all areas that will be supported by *The Right Start to Phonics* – be it Maths, Understanding the World or Expressive Arts and Design.

Commonality between all EYFS documentation

The points that follow are common across all EYFS documentation and are important as we think specifically about Early Phonics:

- The Statutory framework and non-statutory documents all make reference to **Early Phonics**

- The non-statutory frameworks demonstrate homogenous learning across the EYFS. This supports the purpose of *The Right Start to Phonics* and the included activities

- The adult role is crucial to support children to tune into sound

A word about inclusivity

I would like to add, not as an afterthought but because it is an assumptive thread that runs naturally through all the activities I have included, that they have been designed to be inclusive of the majority of diverse needs one might come across in the Early Years.

Some of the activities will broadly suit our youngest children, whilst others will be more suitable for older children, some of the board games, for example. The activities can, therefore, be selected for any child's individual learning needs; whether these are a diagnosed special educational need or otherwise. In addition to this, each activity includes ideas for making adaptations and adjustments whether this is for the individual child or perhaps with the resources or space you have at your disposal.

This inclusion is also about the situation and the adult who might be supporting the child. The information and activities can be available for a broad variety of contexts, including parents who are home-schooling their children, parents who are travelling, play therapists or teachers in hospitals where children of all ages might be missing school learning for varying lengths of time, parents wanting to support their children with home learning in addition to any other settings they might attend. Then of course, those practitioners who are teaching children in a variety of settings such as childminders, pre-schools, nurseries, after-school clubs and children in schools.

Points to peruse and ponder . . .

■ Have you looked at the non-statutory frameworks and perhaps The Reading Framework to support your understanding of early reading/phonics?

■ How do you provide ways to promote children's executive function to support their early reading development and learning? Could some of the activities provide more options?

■ Are you considering how early reading skills/early phonics opportunities can be developed through all areas of learning across the EYFS e.g. Literacy, Maths, Understanding the World, etc.?

References

DfE. 2021. "Development Matters – Non-Statutory Curriculum Guidance for the Early Years Foundation Stage." Accessed August 2023. https://assets.publishing.service.gov.uk

DfE. 2023. *Statutory Framework for the Early Years Foundation Stage.* London: DfE.

Early Education. 2021. "Birth to 5 Matters: Non Statutory Guidance for the EYFS." Accessed August 2023. https://early-education.org.uk/product/birth-to-5-matters-non-statutory-guidance-for-the-eyfs/

Early Years Coalition. 2021. *Birth to 5 Matters.* St Albans: Early Education.

Education Endowment Foundation. 2021. Accessed June 2023. https://educationendowment foundation.org.uk/education-evidence/teaching-learning-toolkit/parental-engagement#:~:text=By%20designing%20and%20delivering%20effective,specific%20skills%2C%20such%20as%20reading.

Goswami, Usha. 2014. *Child Psychology, A Very Short Introduction.* Oxford: Oxford University Press.

Grenier, Julian. 2020. *Working with the Revised Early Years Foundation Stage: Principles into Practice.* London: Sheringham Nursery School and Children's Centre.

Pound, Linda. 2005. *How Children Learn.* London: Step Forward Publishing.

UNICEF. 1989. "United Nations Convention of the Rights of the Child." Accessed June 2023. www.unicef.org.uk/what-we-do/un-convention-child-rights/

2 Research into Early Phonics

In this chapter

In this chapter, we delve into some research about early learning and how this impacts Early Phonics:

- From babies through to children at the end of the EYFS, we look into how language develops and embeds itself in a child's memory

- We then think about memory itself and its imperative importance when learning to read

- Theories about how children learn to read are reflected upon in the light of Early Phonics, establishing the importance of this earliest element of the phonic reading process

- Executive functions and how they are useful for Early Phonics learning are explored in more depth as well as being developed by the activities

It is important for practitioners to understand and be able to share with confidence the 'why' of what they do. This chapter will enable such conversations.

Research into early phonics – listening skills

Teaching children to read using a phonetic system is not new; however, teaching reading using this method has drifted in and out of favour in England over time. When learning to read, the realisation for a child that they can perform this act autonomously provides one of their first and most significant milestones. It offers them independence and freedom, with their world expanding exponentially before their eyes. Teaching children to read using a phonic approach can offer this for many children and often

DOI: 10.4324/9781003451082-4

with surprising rapidity. For other children, it may take more time for the learning to become embedded, but the fact that it does happen is the part that is vitally important.

Phonics as a foundation for reading – those nuts and bolts!

Although I am clearly a proponent of phonics as a method of teaching children to read, I am certainly pragmatic about it and realise that it is not a 'one size fits all' approach, although it works for the vast majority of children. In addition to this, it needs to be noted that phonics are the 'nuts and bolts' of reading. The first part to be learnt that will hold all the skills together. There are a great deal of other elements that need to come together for a child to become a competent, confident, happy, lifelong reader.

The ability to listen

The first of these elements is what this book is fundamentally about. Early phonics: the foundations of later phonemic learning based in auditory discrimination and the ability to use these skills effectively and purposefully.

A gift for all

For many children, this is a natural part of their early growth, but it cannot be taken for granted that this will be so for all children. To ensure children have an even platform from which to launch their reading, we should provide learning opportunities based on listening. We need to close the reading gap to ensure all children have the opportunity to succeed. Alex Quigley (2020) says in his book *Closing the Reading Gap*, that reading 'is not just a means to other ends. It is an end in itself that proves one of the greatest of rewards for living' (p. 14). Being able to read will open up a world not only of successful opportunities for life, for a career in any chosen path but also a world of learning and enjoyment. Reading is nourishing as a pastime and to find out about your world and about other people. It encourages you to think, to challenge, to imagine and to know. It also supports mental health, transporting one to another place, moving one's mind from its current space and reducing anxiety. Hence, ensuring that all children can do this successfully is the greatest gift we can give them.

Our need for memory

Although being able to hear sounds is extremely important, it is not just this simple skill alone that will effectively support early reading. An article by Emma Spiers (2023) discusses auditory memory, specifically how the improvement of this skill helps a child's blending skills. Here, she explains that it's not enough just to be able to hear the sounds, but as an executive function, it's about the ability to hold those sounds in your memory, access them when needed and have the additional skill to be able to place them together as words.

Spiers quite rightly points out that nowadays, we are required to remember information much more rarely than we did in the past. Phone numbers and other such information do not need to be committed to memory because we have easy electronic access to search engines, maps, addresses and previous 'e-message' conversations. Our forebears needed considerably more information to be committed to memory, including addresses and numbers, but also other things, such as traditional tales to be told to children from memory, rhymes and songs. This will indicate that our predecessors possessed a more robustly developed functioning memory through necessity. It can be presumed that this will be something we are progressively going to become less reliant upon.

The ability to hold information

For this reason, telling stories, making them up and retelling them is a crucial part of early literacy. It will help to develop executive function with children needing to hold information in their heads. Storytelling is arguably a necessary part of brain development, an exercise in encouraging and activating lesser-used parts of our brains to function. It is interesting to think how our brains might be physically changing in structure as we need to remember less, and research into this phenomenon is already being undertaken. A recent thought-provoking article by Rebecca Seal (2022) noted that 'digital amnesia', which is a description of changes in the way our memories function, due to our reliance on digital technology is a recognised concern. Perhaps this can be addressed and established to some extent in the EYFS through children remembering stories, rhymes and songs. It is clearly a very necessary skill to support the use of phonics.

How do we learn best?

A book that was introduced to me during the 1980s was entitled *How children learn* by John Holt (1967). This was updated recently and, in the context of a career in early education, the book seems to encapsulate a phrase from teacher training in that previous decade: 'discovery learning'.

This seems fundamental to early learning and has evolved and become the reason we now like to ensure that children are taught or have skills modelled for them and then are left to explore them in their own independent learning time. This also implies that the learning should be active and is fortunately fundamental to all of the Early Phonics activities in this book.

Discovering something for oneself is a guaranteed way of ensuring that learning is embedded. If I were taught to change a car tyre, I know for sure that I would remember little if I had simply watched somebody else doing it (which is, in fact, what has happened!).

Interest, pedagogy and Isaac Newton

Holt's idea is that children come to learning when they are interested in it, including when children are learning to read. This made sense when taken in the same mode of thinking as Cliff Moon and Moran (1975) and his approach to children learning to read. I believe this was the way it had been suggested that we, as trainee teachers, were to teach early reading.

To take an element of this approach, it was the 'tobacco tin' of words that a child would be given that I remembered clearly, but these would only be words that the child was interested in. I might now choose to disagree with some of the elements of these approaches, but I am grateful to these predecessors of mine because their research and ideas have all helped to create my own pedagogy. In the words of Isaac Newton, we are all 'standing on the shoulders of giants'!

I understand that learning will be heightened if each child is taught only what they are interested in at the time they demonstrated that interest. This would work well in certain circumstances, potentially for someone who has chosen to 'home school' their child, but would be challenging to deliver in a class of 30 unique children within an education system with prescribed 'goals'.

John Holt describes a girl whom he knows desperately wanting to read (because she was acutely aware that family members around her could all do this and she herself couldn't), but he explains how she will do it in her own time when she's reading 'in her own way'.

He continued to explain that this would happen naturally because she would be in a literacy rich environment, which seems fundamental to this approach. Ensuring you have a 'literacy rich' environment is going to positively impact all children's early reading experiences.

This creating a literacy-rich environment for children is also an easy way to redress imbalances for those who do not receive this at home, as the girl Holt describes was clearly fortunate enough to have. She was richly surrounded by books, newspapers, magazines and, vitally, family members who were avid readers.

He talks about the importance of children's exposure to letters, their purpose and their shape, for example, before they come anywhere near them in a formal context. This exposure will lead to children more authentically gaining confidence in their knowledge of literacy, and it will become more established the more they are exposed to it. As a principle of 'discovery learning', the more children 'come across' something, the more established the learning becomes, hence the importance of repetition. I wouldn't disagree with this, and I talk more specifically about how to create a 'literacy rich' space in the chapter on The Learning Environment.

As I mentioned before, there are elements from these philosophies that resonate strongly with current high-quality Early Years practice and engaging children in Early Phonics. However, as a Reception class teacher, teaching in this very individualised way is not always possible, especially when we are thinking of reading. Although, with a well-considered approach to the way you teach and the timing of that, you can be fairly certain of a) getting it right for most children and b) knowing really well which children will need further support and what that might look like. This book, with the guidance and activities provided, will hopefully offer support for all 'teachers', whether one-to-one or for a larger group.

A matter of questions

Holt continues with his theme on children learning to read. He says it is preferable for a child to ask you questions about a book rather than the adult constantly asking the child questions. I understand the way he is explaining these situations arising over time, and it is perfectly plausible that this would happen with a child in a home learning environment. But how could we encourage this as part and parcel of a busier learning environment with a larger number of children? This thought process and the asking of questions has become one of the early reading activities I share in Part Two of this book. Not only will this support the development of early reading skills, but also elements of executive function and the Characteristics of Effective Learning.

Challenging books

Another element that Holt talks about is one that I am very keen to promote. This is that children love books that are actually too hard for them to understand completely. Don't feel you need to limit children to books that are promoted as being within their specific 'age range'. If you are reading a more complex book to a child, it will bathe them in language that is too hard for them to understand completely. However, children adore 'hard' words and complicated language. Let them imagine what the word might mean or explain it if they are interested. Children engaging with stories that are read to them in this way are again adding to their developing listening skills and knowledge of sounds and vocabulary. I can remember my mother explaining the meaning of 'soporific' when reading *The Tale of the Flopsy Bunnies* by Beatrix Potter (1909) to me. I doubt it became part of my regular vocabulary at age 4, but I loved remembering what it meant each time the story was re-read to me. Then I can remember my own son only wanting me to read the original version of *Jungle Book* to him when he was really quite small. I wondered at his focus as I read the very old-fashioned language of Rudyard Kipling, but he loved the story, and it always did the job of getting him off to sleep.

Expression is vital

Holt firmly believed that reading with expression was the key to supporting understanding. It is good now that in the updated *Ofsted School Inspection Handbook*

(September 2023), it is expected that adults reading to children should do so with expertise and knowledge, reading interestingly and with expression to the children: 'Staff read to children in a way that excites and engages them, introducing new ideas, concepts and vocabulary'. Again, this excitement built by an adult will aid a child's focus and intense listening, engaging them in the story.

Books without words

Clearly abundant expression should happen when reading books *with* words, but we must not forget the all-important books without words. All-important because these books offer so many incredible opportunities to children who have not begun to read independently yet or those who are still in the early stages of reading.

You could share a book without words or even an interesting picture or painting. The lack of text should not mean that expression is forgotten or that a rich vocabulary is ignored. These two vital elements of reading must be included and can add so much fun for both the expert/adult reader and the child.

How they might be approached

The vocabulary or storyline can be the same each time – this will encourage the listener to join in expertly after a few times of listening, or it can equally be changed each time. This could be from one or two words to the entire story. A word or two changing will potentially elicit shrieks of delight from the child when you have made a 'mistake', and this will encourage the use of auditory memory. Children have to listen intently to spot the mistakes to catch you out! The characters' names could stay the same or change, and the setting or the beginning of the story could be the same or different – so many to choose from: 'Once upon a time . . .', 'One dark night in the middle of Winter . . .', 'Bang! and Splash! were the first things they heard . . . !'

These books offer so many glorious options for fun. This can then lead to opportunities that extend to the child joining in and then taking over the reins. You could model effective listening, and then you could take your turn to ask them what happens, what happens next and where they would like the story to go.

Books with no words support children in seeing themselves as readers. There are no limitations of accuracy, understanding phonics, digraphs and trigraphs; there is simply a love of language to be developed and nurtured.

Listening to the language around us

Usha Goswami (2014), in her book *Child Psychology, a very short introduction*, interestingly talks about our national sensitivity to sounds from our native languages. In our early months of life, the brain organises the sounds we need and becomes accustomed to hearing them.

Figure 2.1 A photo of a pregnant lady reading a children's book.
Source: Photograph taken by the author

Goswami describes this understanding of the sounds in a native language as 'categorical perception'. We, in turn, then learn to make these sounds ourselves, and we learn to broadly recognise them, too, as we come across other people who may say these sounds slightly differently, we categorise them instinctively – fabulous instinct for tuning into sound.

Speaking to babies

Prior to this, Goswami discusses sound patterns. The idea of Infant Directed Speech (IDS) is discussed. This is the tuneful way we talk to babies that is vital for them, as it enables them to tune into language. This IDS supports the rhythmic parts of speech that are reflected so clearly in Early Phonics.

It is very interesting to learn that IDS helps children to learn that our language, whichever language that might be, is not just one long continuous sound. This rhythmic speech teaches children where words begin and end.

In the Early Years classroom, we can also see the value of this for children who are learning to read and write – the recognition that speech is actually divided up into individual words. The reason IDS teaches this skill is because when speaking in this way, we instinctively stress the syllables, particularly the first. Listen to yourself or someone else when they speak to a baby and see if you hear the very distinctive intonation. Perhaps say out loud, 'Shall we go to the sea-side?' as if saying it enthusiastically to a very small baby. Did you have the stress on 'SEA'? Hopefully, you did, to demonstrate the point.

In addition to this, IDS also serves to gain the attention of babies. Goswami (2014) continues that, apparently, it has been proven that babies actually prefer it to other forms of adult speech. If you spend time with our youngest children, take the opportunity to use IDS. If you work with older children, be mindful of the playful nature of speech. Songs, rhymes and poems are all of equal importance, as are conversation and commentary, a naturally warm and immersive use of language.

A reason to sing!

Another feature of learning sound patterns in this way, Goswami tell us, is that there are 'statistical clues that tell small children which sounds belong together and make words' (p. 42). This is fascinating and demonstrates a real focus on the clear and sensical order of letters to make words in the language the child is exposed to.

Further, this finding ties into the executive function of holding concepts in your mind, the working memory that is so vital for early phonological and phonemic awareness and learning.

A joyful fact that Goswami shares with us is that if the 'statistical stream' is sung to the child, then the learning is actually much more 'efficient'. So, there we have a great reason to sing with young children!

A strong phonic connection

More research from Goswami (2014) that links strongly to Early Phonics is again about babies. It has been found that, from their earliest months, babies possess the cognitive awareness to take part in a conversation. Of course, this doesn't start with a speech link, but some 'grunting-type sounds' might be heard, and some vowel-based 'comfort' sounds would be decipherable, which sounds more akin to speech. This apparently evolves at around seven months of age when proper babbling sounds are then discernible and are more commonly heard. Very interestingly, again, Goswami tells us that research has shown that adults can distinguish between babbles from their own language as opposed to other languages due to the 'rhythmic structure' of the babbles! That indicates a heightened ability of very young children to discriminate between sounds and that they possess the ability to generate familiar ones.

Phonological knowledge

As we speak and listen to spoken language, phonological knowledge isn't obvious to us at all, although it is such a very necessary requirement of both reading and writing. It is something that needs to be taught.

This is taught as 'phonological awareness', which is helping children to hear sounds in words, to identify rhymes or even words that actually don't rhyme at all! Goswami explains that 'The relationship between phonological awareness and reading development is found in all of the world's languages, not just in languages that use the alphabet'. A child's ability to use their phonological awareness effectively, to hear rhymes, for example, is an indication of how well, quickly or effectively a child will learn to read. Therefore, the activities and knowledge shared in this book will be vital in gauging a child's readiness to read, fully supporting this process. Goswami (2014) agrees that rhymes with, for example, steady beats or pulses are all positive additions for a wholesome grounding in Early Phonics, looking towards an outcome of effective reading in the future. 'Given a strong oral language phonological foundation, and good oral language skills, most children will learn the alphabetic code quite quickly, and will be able to recode simple regularly spelled words to sound during the first year of schooling'!

Skills that need to come before the phonic code

Some more information about Early Phonics comes in an interesting book by Sally Neaum, entitled *What comes before phonics* (2017). She argues that although it is broadly accepted that phonological awareness is a prerequisite to being able to access phonics effectively, there is still some debate and ongoing research into the finer points of this relationship. Neaum reflects on how 'phonological awareness is the ability to focus on aspects of language other than their meaning – aspects of language such as rhyme, or clapping out syllables, or identifying words with the same initial sound' (p. 140). Phonological awareness is, therefore, about the larger parts of words rather than the individual sounds within them. Phonemic awareness, however, is a focus on those smaller parts of words i.e. the sounds. Children need to be able to identify and manipulate these sounds to be able to use them for reading and writing. This is the skill I am focusing on in this book. Children learn and embed these skills before they start to learn the phonic code. Neaum explains that to hone these skills effectively, 'children need opportunities to listen carefully – quiet times when they can attend to and absorb language'.

Specifics of phonological awareness

In Neaum's chapter looking at Phonological Awareness, she explains that 'the earliest aspect of Phonological Awareness is the ability to hear rhymes and alliteration ability'. From experience, I would agree with this to a certain extent, although I think that this certainly can be one of the last skills to develop. I have experience of it taking a lot of repetition of activities and games for this skill to be embedded for some children and a great deal of other listening games to enable them to tune into sound effectively and efficiently. As with writing and making anti-clockwise circles, it is great for those who embed this early. For others, it needs frequent revisiting.

Neaum explained earlier in her book that children master these skills at different rates, as they should as unique individuals. We all tread our own path, and rates of mastery will differ. She talks about getting children to 'tune into' rhyme and alliteration as early as possible in their lives. I agree and am hoping that the strategies and activities

I am sharing will build a robust foundation for this by encouraging children to tune into sound.

Honing executive functions

Reflecting again on the homogenous traits of early learning, something that has come into the consciousness of the teaching profession during my time as a teacher is the notion of executive function (Marcie Yeager and Daniel Yeager 2013). We have explored a 'working memory' that is vital to a child to be able to use the phonic approach to learn to read and write (and undoubtedly most of their other lifelong learning to follow).

Activities such as rhyming games will unequivocally support a developing working memory, with a child holding a rhyme in their head, e.g. the word 'cat', and adding something they have heard before to create that rhyme, e.g. 'bat'. They could even be adding something less obvious and more abstract by creating a 'nonsense word' that creates that rhyme, using other information that has been embedded previously, and come up with 'zat'.

Other executive functions

There are other executive functions that can also support or are supported by Early Phonics.

'*Response Inhibition*' is another executive function to be honed. This is where a child might be presented with things that will interfere with what they might have been about to do, therefore requiring them to delay their response. Taking part in turn-taking games and following rules will support this development.

The ability to '*shift focus*' from one thing to something different is another executive function. Again, following rules in simple games, singing a broad range of nursery rhymes, listening to several poems or stories and using puppets or other props to retell a favourite story will all support this.

It takes little imagination to realise that '*cognitive flexibility*' is a function that will enable a child to employ phonic strategies effectively across all of their learning. This executive function is about finding different ways of doing things, which is such a huge element of the EYFS overall, particularly with the Characteristics of Effective Learning. Children will naturally rehearse this function in a rich, stimulating, well-prepared learning environment. The teaching of strategies, playing games and learning to stay with an activity until it is finished all provide the right climate to practice cognitive flexibility. Therefore, you can see the connection between the games and activities that support Early Phonics in this book.

The last executive function I will mention is '*goal orientation*'. This concerns what might be 'multi-step plans' where a goal is to be achieved. As noted previously, sticking with an activity, even when presented with challenges, will support the development of this function. This will establish the desire to complete something and the intrinsic satisfaction that it brings, such as completing a game or activity.

But what if it doesn't work?

I recently dipped into a book by Christopher Such (2021) called *The Art and Science of Teaching Primary Reading*. He, quite early in the book, asks a question that I must admit I think about and discuss quite frequently, 'What if it doesn't work?' – meaning the conventional, phonic-driven method of teaching children to read. His answer is that some other strategies, such as teaching comprehension more robustly, might help. However, 'there is no escaping the fact that competence in reading depends on fluent decoding'. From John Holt to Christopher Such, there comes the recognition that phonics might not be THE ONLY way to teach reading, but most theorists seem to acknowledge that phonics do have a part to play in most reading strategies.

Such continues to say that 'fluent decoding in turn depends on a student's knowledge of the common sound-spelling correspondences of English and the skills relating to phonemic awareness' (2021). It is this last part that I'm interested in. Skills in phonemic awareness will only develop effectively if phonological awareness is honed. This is the vital foundation that must not be overlooked.

Points to peruse and ponder . . .

- Can you remember being taught to read? What system was used at the time?

- What is your opinion on using the phonic approach to teaching children to read?

- Are you able to explain why you value (or don't value!) the importance of teaching Early Phonics?

- Have you analysed which children you work with need additional Early Phonic support, and have you identified exactly what that support might be?

- Do you think you are exposing children regularly to rich and ambitious language which will support the development of their vocabulary?

- Have you considered how you might promote the development of executive functions?

- Do you currently use any activities that discretely support a child's working memory? Do you have any ideas for games or activities that might support children's working memory?

References

Goswami, Usha. 2014. *Child Psychology, A Very Short Introduction*. Oxford: Oxford University Press.

Holt, John. 1967. *How Children Learn*. London: Penguin.

Moon, Cliff, and Bridie Moran. 1975. *A Question of Reading*. London: Macmillan.

Neaum, Sally. 2017. *What Comes Before Phonics?* London: Sage.

Potter, Beatrix. 1909. *The Tale of the Flopsy Bunnies*. Frederick Warne & Co School Inspection Handbook. Accessed May 2023. www.gov.uk/government/publications/school-inspection-handbook-eif/school-inspection-handbook-for-september-2023#grade-descriptors-for-early-years-provision-in-schools

Quigley, Alex. 2020. *Closing the Reading Gap*. Oxon: Routledge.

Seal, Rebecca. Accessed November 6, 2023. www.theguardian.com/global/2022/jul/03/is-your-smartphone-ruining-your-memory-the-rise-of-digital-amenesia

Spiers, Emma. Accessed April 6, 2023. www.teachearlyyears.com/learning-and-development/view/auditory-memory-blending-skills

Such, Christopher. 2021. *The Art and Science of Teaching Primary Reading*. London: Sage Education Endowment Foundation. Accessed July 2023. https://educationendowmentfoundation.org.uk/education-evidence/teaching-learning-toolkit/phonics

Yeager, Marcie, and Daniel Yeager. 2013. *Executive Function and Child Development*. London: W. W. Norton and Company.

3 The adult and Early Phonics

In this chapter

The vital role the adult plays in ensuring that Early Phonics is taught and presented to young children effectively is explored, including:

■ What children need to be in place to ensure they hone their auditory skills

■ What some of their barriers to this learning might be and what we, as adults, can do to help address them

■ Some thoughts about phonics are shared by current practitioners who are working with children in the EYFS

■ The idea that Early Phonics has no specific endpoint and that the skills should continue to be honed is explored

■ Early phonics and early reading skills will be supported by adults reading to and with children. Effective methods of doing this are shared

The adult role in Early Phonics

Where to start?

The role of the adult in supporting the development of skills in Early Phonics is clearly critical. From the earliest days after birth, it is crucial that children are exposed to language and sounds in abundance. Many children will naturally pick up this auditory discrimination, developing an awareness of the sounds around them in their environment. This will give them a fabulous, burgeoning foundation for their later literacy learning.

DOI: 10.4324/9781003451082-5

However, some children will not be so fortunate for an abundance of reasons. To ensure that all children have an even platform from which to start their phonic journey, the adult in the EYFS must be the catalyst for ensuring equality for all. Getting to know the children is imperative. Understanding each individual, unique child. Informal assessments made during playful activities, conversation and playing alongside young children will give adults ample opportunity to understand how much language a child has and will give insights into each child's ability to both hear and listen to sounds around them. Whatever their starting point, all children need to be engaging in Early Phonics activities supported by confident and knowledgeable adults.

Once children start in a Reception class, they are expected to 'hit the carpet running', as it were, as the fast-paced phonics teaching starts immediately. This demonstrates very loudly to me the vital importance of ensuring our children are as ready as they can possibly be to be able to take this pace of learning on board. The only way they will be able to do this is if their phonological skills are well-developed in readiness for this statutory requirement.

With this requirement in mind, the area of Early Phonics was discussed with some experienced Early Years practitioners and leaders who kindly shared their responses to their own current phonics teaching.

Barriers to learning

All of the skills in Early Phonics are vital, but a child's interaction with these skills needs to form a playful part of their early learning. It is down to the adults to establish a child's readiness for learning and what strategies might be used to ensure that learning is approached in an appropriate way.

An observation from Charlotte B, an Early Years teacher, about her current Reception class and the requirement for phonics learning was that she is increasingly finding that

> too many children begin school so dysregulated that they need a long time to learn how to manage their feelings and their sense of self. They don't need the added pressure of sitting on the carpet for 20 minutes trying to focus on a screen or resource held by the teacher.

Children with additional needs

The 20-minute session is a requirement in a Reception class and can be seen in some instances being delivered to children who are not ready for this style of learning, never mind the content of the session. Their lack of 'readiness' may be due to self-regulation challenges for the child or because they have Special Educational Needs or Disabilities (SEND). This means that their experiences and skills in Early Phonics are likely to be limited.

Charlotte A is a teacher in an inner-city school and is concerned that this is the case with her current phonic scheme. She explains, 'There does still seem to be a gap for supporting those with less foundational understanding of sounds, literally the sounds we hear around us each day'.

Support with speech and language delays

Donna, who teaches a mixed-year group that includes Reception-aged children, agreed and made a valid point about the children who were making slower progress in phonics. The common theme for these children was special education needs, particularly those with Speech and Language delays. These children were struggling particularly with the blending and segmenting sounds they were being taught.

'Without the ability to blend, their phonic knowledge has very little use and this can be a bit of a barrier to some children'. She felt there was 'limited support and guidance around Speech and Language development connected to phonics despite how closely linked the two areas are'.

How to help

My advice would be that the activities shared in this book would be a good starting point. They would greatly help and offer some support for all these children, alongside other specialist support. The children would benefit hugely from time spent helping them to develop their auditory discrimination and working memory.

Targeted work in small groups

Whatever the reason for a lack of foundational understanding, working with these children individually or in small groups will support their learning needs. This is why the activities in this book are invaluable, giving opportunities for these children to explore the foundations needed in an appropriate learning environment for them. Short bursts of activity will ensure that shorter attention spans are catered for. The range in complexity of the activities will also ensure that children's individual needs are well supported in all elements of Early Phonics so the age of the child can be responded to.

The great outdoors

Some children are predisposed to learn more effectively when outdoors.

The outdoor environment offers freedom. A child's senses will tune into the different sensations of sound, smell and the atmosphere. The activities have been created so many can be used both indoors and in an outdoor learning environment, so children who learn more readily in either of these spaces will be able to do so.

English as an additional language

From further discussion with Charlotte A, one 'wish' that she has is that there might be more support for those children for whom English is not their first language.

A 'way in' to phonics for these children is provided with the activities suggested in this book. Children amaze us with the speed at which they take a new language on board. A foundation in these Early Phonic skills, through the activities, would have the added advantage of exposing these children to more informal conversation and a playful exposure to English. For these children, learning should also be offered in a tangible, multi-sensory way. This is a broadly acknowledged pedagogy in the EYFS and a theory expounded by Maria Montessori, amongst others (Pound 2007). These children would definitely benefit from the playful activities in Early Phonics shared in Part Two of this book.

Closing gaps

The categories in this book, Sounds Around, Sounds We Make and Sounds with Words, offer a very broad range of Early Phonic skills and create opportunities for informal assessments to be made in order to establish where the children's learning needs to be pitched. If children already have well-developed skills in an area, the focus can then become directed towards other categories. Even if a child has a developing competence in all the areas, they will still benefit from experiencing the activities because so many other EYFS skills will also be supported e.g. social skills, turn-taking, communication and language skills, broadening vocabulary, early maths skills – the Characteristics of Effective Learning.

But very importantly, if a child is not clearly experienced or is not developing skills generally in their auditory awareness, this can become a focus for their individual learning to ensure gaps are closed from the earliest opportunity. The activities can become part of their daily routine both in their setting and for home learning to ensure the early skills are developed and embedded.

How Early Phonics continues

When considering the point that children are expected to be at when starting in a Reception class, where the statutory phonics teaching is taking place, this could be seen as the 'end point' for Early Phonics. It is certainly the point at which, ideally, the foundations should be fully prepared and can gradually be built upon. However, it is still vitally important that Early Phonics continues from this point for it to be the 'safety net' that is essential to underpin all phonic learning and a child's continuing journey towards fluent reading and writing. Children will continue to come across challenging elements of phonics and reading that will be all the easier to decipher if they can draw upon this early learning. They need to retain their familiarity with rhyme and alliteration. The playful nature of language they engage with in Early Phonics will ensure that important elements can still be drawn upon throughout their early reading experiences. This will ensure that new words and phrases are approached with strategies borne out of established knowledge rather than simply guesswork.

Independent access to Early Phonics

As part of this continuing connection with Early Phonics, activities in this book can easily be left available for the children to access independently, perhaps in the form of an interactive display or a selection of baskets or boxes containing resources for the activities. Following the direct 'teaching' of the game or activity, the children could then hone their skills further by playing the game again when they choose. A game that is fun, they understand and they can play with their friends is likely to be regularly accessed.

Lisa, an experienced practitioner and EYFS leader, discussed this. She is aware that her experience enables her to provide this for her children. She is also acutely aware that a new or inexperienced practitioner might not have the confidence and experience to draw from to 'tweak' learning to match the needs of a diverse cohort of young children and to provide activities for independent use. This book would, therefore, undoubtedly provide support for such practitioners.

Efficient use of time

Time is precious in the EYFS, so it needs to be used purposefully for both adults and children. The activities in this book will ensure adults can quickly use the resources to create an 'enhancement' to their learning environment that will target specific skills for specific children. The children will clearly benefit from this enhancement by being able to access it during their child-initiated learning time, bolstering and embedding previous learning. If adults are providing this, it is essential that it is 'signposted' or introduced to the children prior to their child-initiated learning so they are aware of the activity. This will promote its use.

Support for parents with home learning

Another huge benefit of the activities is that they can be shared with parents who could access them for home learning. The activities are simple to use, and the important sections with each activity of 'Why' and 'Making other connections' will clarify for parents the reasons they are being asked to support their children and precisely how the activities will benefit their child and their learning.

Lisa, an Early Years Leader, explains that something missing from her current phonics scheme is support for parents that aligns with the ethos in their EYFS. Their current scheme offers only electronic or paper-based activities: 'It would be better to have ideas for games, etc., for parents e.g. going on a sound hunt or looking for letters on road signs when out on a walk'. These are exactly the type of interactive, engaging activities that are included in Part Two of *The Right Start to Phonics*, making them ideal for home learning.

Figure 3.1 A photograph of an adult and child talking beside a river.
Source: Photograph taken by the author

Making Early Phonics interactive

Playful, meaningful learning

I am extremely passionate about learning being interactive, and I believe that we should be engaging children physically in all learning wherever possible. Children learn best when their learning is active, fun, tuned into their current learning needs, engages them, is interesting and when they feel like a part of the experience. Passively sitting back and being expected to receive knowledge is not going to work for the majority of children, especially not when they are very young when they are learning in the EYFS. Nonetheless, there will be times for 'adult-led' sessions where an adult is imparting knowledge, explaining, modelling and demonstrating skills; however, this can all be undertaken in a 'playful' way.

Play and Early Phonics

The principle will be the same when you are working with children on Early Phonics activities, in whichever setting you might be working with them. This could be your child in your home, as a parent, a play therapist in a hospital, a childminder, a preschool or nursery; the children will all learn best by being active. This may be limited by the children's own individual circumstances; for example, a child in hospital may well be limited by the amount of activity they can take on, but sitting fairly still to play the activities shouldn't mean that they are not still playful in nature.

Actively revisiting learning

As an example, in the EYFS Statutory Framework (DfE 2023), in the Communication and Language educational programme, it states that 'Reading frequently to children, and engaging them **actively** in stories, non-fiction, rhymes and poems, and then providing them with extensive opportunities to use and embed . . . [the learning] will give children the opportunity to thrive'. The key word here is 'actively', and this clearly applies also to other early literacy-related learning.

The DfE acknowledge the vital importance of those extensive opportunities to embed the learning – this will be through the children actively accessing that learning independently at a later time. They might be playing a game using the resources you have left for them, revisiting a book you have previously shared or playing with some nursery rhyme props to sing the rhymes to themselves or with a friend or parent. The opportunities need to be there for the children to engage in this revisiting of previous learning actively.

There is a second key word for me in that quote from the Statutory Framework: 'thrive'. If you are reading this book, you are clearly invested in our children thriving because you want the very best start for them on their reading journey – that lifelong skill that is going to make a difference to them thriving in society and the wider world.

The importance of reading

The heading might seem a little obvious, especially as this entire book is about the very start of the journey of children's learning to read, so clearly, it is important. However, I am not thinking of the children here but more of the adults. Firstly, this is about the importance of children being 'read to', of them being exposed to language and stories from birth, or even before. As Alex Quigley (2020) explains, humans have only been reading for around 5,000 years. The process is certainly one that must be learnt in

Figure 3.2 A photo of an Early Years learning environment.
Source: Photo taken by author

some way; it is not something that happens naturally as with walking or talking. This is because the neural pathways have not become sufficiently developed to make this a natural process.

Books from birth

If children have books shared with them from birth, they are hearing so many more words than those children who are not read to. As well as the richness of the vocabulary they are hearing, they are listening to the nuances of language, the pauses, the intonation, the way stories work, that stories have a beginning, middle and an end, that some sounds and some words might be heard over and again, others feature just once. They will begin to understand that if a story is repeated over and over, it will always be the same – the same words, similar intonation. You just need to think about the story of The Three Little Pigs and how countless retellings will always have the wolf saying, 'I'll huff, and I'll puff, and I'll ***blow*** your house down!' with exactly the same inflection. This repetitiveness will become embedded and create a foundation for understanding language and how it works.

Adults being seen as 'readers'

Another strand of the role of the adult in early reading comes as part of our role in enveloping children in a rich literacy environment. It is crucial that adults are seen to read by children, showing children that reading is both useful, necessary and fun! Adults modelling reading for entertainment in a home learning environment, reading for pleasure instead of watching television, is perhaps an option. In a school or setting, this is less easy to do, but having a selection of adult books obviously placed for you to explain their purpose to the children might be a simple but positive addition to your environment. Model the use of dictionaries to the children when the opportunity arises. If you have a short time for children to quietly 'read' or to look at books, spend some time acknowledging the children's reading, but model your own reading at this time, too! Tell the children why you are enjoying your book! This will add immense value to the skill of reading, for the children to actually see an adult reading for pleasure. It will also reinforce the idea of reading being a lifelong, pleasurable activity

Children who are disadvantaged and vulnerable

Quigley also reminds us that children who are read to regularly will, by the time they are 5 years old, have heard in excess of a million more words than those children who are not read to. We need to be mindful always of the fact that these rich literacy experiences are not happening for all children. There are those disadvantaged and vulnerable children who will not have books in their homes and will not have all of the experiences mentioned previously. In our schools and settings, we need to be providing this richness for these children in an endeavour to close the reading gap.

Connections for pre-readers

In the context of Early Phonics, the more real word sounds children hear, the more connections they make, creating links between sounds and words that feature in their home language. This is what Early Phonics is about; it is the preparation of the children's auditory skills and their learning to use them to read and write. Establishing a literacy-rich environment is a great preparation for all phonic learning.

Book and story-sharing

Sharing books with young children will obviously evolve as the children's skills and abilities grow, and they will, therefore, engage differently. The length of time they can focus and become engaged in the pictures, as well as the words, will gradually grow as their own spoken language also develops. Small children will love the comfort and cosiness of being cuddled as they are read to. This is vital to encourage a love of reading. If the child is emotionally enriched from the experience of being read to and feels love and warmth from the adult, this will provide a bedrock from which their lifelong love of reading will be launched.

The 'act' of reading aloud

It is also important that the 'way' the story is read is enriching. That the book is known by the adult is important to make the reading of the story fluid and fluent. The adult needs to 'act' a little when reading to make it interesting for the child or children who are listening, so practicing might be a good idea if, as an adult, you are not confident. It is so easy to record yourself reading a story nowadays, so give it a go! See if you entertain yourself with your reading aloud.

As children begin to read

An important part of the broad process of a child learning to read is when they practice and read aloud to an adult. This might be a book with simple words or even a book with no words. The principle is the same, and the role of the adult in this is vital.

Figure 3.3 A photograph of an adult reading a child's book.
Source: Photograph taken by the author

The art of listening to children read

In the context of supporting children with their reading, it is crucial that the adult is fully engaged in this activity and is distracted by things happening around them as little as possible. This is often hard to achieve, particularly in a busy classroom learning environment, but imagine how you would feel if you were reading something out loud to somebody and they were constantly looking at other people, even speaking to other people or looking at their phone . . . just as an example. It would be annoying, but also, think about what message that conveys to the child. That message is that what they are doing is not important; it isn't a priority to you as the valued adult because you are looking and engaging elsewhere.

Asking pertinent questions

For the adult to pay real, focused attention to the child who is reading is so very important. I would add that this is equally important if the child is 'telling' a story from pictures. In their eyes, they are reading to you, so you still need to listen. Asking questions will deepen the child's engagement with the story, but try to make this conversational, natural and authentic. Bombarding a child with superficial or closed questions (those with one-word answers) is going to add very little learning to the

Figure 3.4 A father and son reading together on a sofa.
Source: Photograph taken by the author

experience. Your questions could be ponderings: 'I wonder why the tiger chose to do that?' or 'I don't know how I'd have reacted to that, do you?' as well as some more specific questions about the text, storyline or illustrations.

A recent event

Something unexpected happened recently. I was fortunate enough to be able to visit a local school to 'hear readers'. I was feeling quite excited about being able to do this at long last. I think the appeal was to be able to approach it with a completely different perspective as a 'helper', not a teacher, not an adviser, but just being there to help. There were two huge benefits of doing this that I could see. The first was the time I was able to take. In the two hours I was in the school, I heard just four children read. That meant that I spent a full half hour with each child! This would be nigh on impossible to do on an ordinary day, in an ordinary classroom, as a teacher. The other thing was the complete lack of distraction.

The challenge when hearing children read

When you're in a busy classroom trying to hear a child read one-to-one, you are never able to completely focus on the child, hard as you might try, because there are often 29 other children who need to be on your radar at the same time. When I was teaching, I would always coach the children in my class to understand that they might have to try and sort issues out for themselves if they knew I was reading with a child. That is all part of them becoming independent, using problem-solving strategies and discussing with friends how they might tackle an issue, for example. It is a valuable skill in itself, honing the Characteristics of Effective Learning or the children's executive functions. But, as a teacher, you cannot ever close your mind to everything around you and just focus on one child completely. And try as they might, small children are inevitably egocentric, so interruptions obviously did still happen!

Life as a 'helper'

However, going into school as a 'helper' meant I was released from this pre-occupation and could focus completely on each child, one at a time! It was an edifying experience. When I arrived at the school, I had expected, as an 'Early Years expert' of sorts, to be reading with (or to) the Reception children. It was a surprise to discover that due to the movements of the children on the day, the assistant head teacher asked if I'd mind reading with some Year 3 children instead (who would be 7 or 8 years old). I was happy to help, so, of course, this was fine. The children selected were those who would really benefit from some additional support with reading. What I hadn't expected was the clarity with which I started to see what was missing for these children. The children were all focused and engaged well in their reading. They were all able to access the phonic code but with varying degrees of success, and it became very apparent that some skills were not yet fully developed. To me, the main one was their inability to consistently hold sounds in their head in order to blend them successfully. The children could say each sound individually but then guessed what the word was, usually using the initial sound as an indicator. For example, the word 'beach' might be enunciated as 'boats'. I realised that the work I could do with these children would include some of the activities in this book, to strengthen that skill for them and 'unlock' the power to blend. They needed to develop their working memory.

A matter of questioning

The other skill deficit that struck me was when a child announced that they were going to have 'lots of questions to ask in a minute' as they tapped the open double page of their book! I was looking forward to this with great anticipation as it is one of the activities I have created for the end of *this* book, and I was excited to see how many pertinent questions this child was going to fire at me. What soon became very apparent was that the child had little actual understanding of how to ask a question. What they did was to give me a full verbal description of the pictures on the page interspersed with some conjecture as to what might be about to happen and why. They did this very skilfully with little hesitation. I wondered if this child was very used to answering questions about the books that were being read and the illustrations because this was a frequent process for them during reading sessions. I could see another use for my activities –maybe to share them with parents who might be able to support this skill with home learning.

It's never too late!

It seemed serendipitous that my experience as a reading 'helper' should happen as I am writing about children learning about Early Phonics to be followed by the phonic code. It made me feel that my thoughts were right and that the foundations for learning the phonic code need to be robustly laid. Although, if they aren't, we can still make a difference for our children because it is never too late! Go back to the beginning and fill in those gaps. Those cracks in the foundations can be filled and will enable our children to learn to read with knowledge and fluidity. This will ultimately lead to that great wish we have for them: a lifelong love of reading.

Points to peruse and ponder . . .

- The bottom line is that keeping learning active and engaging will ensure that learning is remembered and that it is fun. Do you think you achieve this?

- What is your current provision for supporting home learning for Early Phonics?

- How could this be developed further?

- How are you plugging the gaps for children who are not yet ready for formal phonics schemes?

- Look back to the chapter about phonics in the EYFS frameworks and remind yourself about the Characteristics of Effective Learning and the importance of play in learning and development for children

- Have you considered the individual starting points for Early Phonics for all of the children you are working with?

- Are you aware of any older primary-aged children who find reading a challenge? If so, consider whether some of the activities in this book could help plug those reading gaps for them

- How are you making the reading experience with children authentic, meaningful and purposeful in these early stages?

- Have you considered how you read aloud to children, i.e. how engagingly you are reading or what questions you are asking and when they are being asked?

References

DfE. 2023. *Statutory Framework for the Early Years Foundation Stage*. London: DfE.
Pound, Linda. 2007. *How Children Learn*. London: Step Forward Publishing.
Quigley, Alex. 2020. *Closing the Reading Gap*. Oxon: Routledge.

4 Phonics across the learning environment

In this chapter

In this chapter, we will look at the importance of the learning environment in supporting Early Phonics. Areas to be considered include:

- The constant, but finely tuned availability of Early Phonic resources in a broad range of learning spaces

- Ensuring that your environment is responsive to the assessments you are making of the children. That these responses adapt over time and suggestions about how what this might look like in your provision

- An extensive table of suggestions of how Early Phonics might be embedded in a high-quality continuous provision

The classroom learning environment

Long before I understood that the environment was the 'third teacher' as described by Loris Malaguzzi, who founded the early schools in Reggio Emilia in Italy (Pound 2007), I loved creating great spaces for the children I was working with. I wanted to create spaces that would inspire, challenge, engage, enthral and would crucially feel to the children within them like a space in which they belonged.

All of those adjectives I have mentioned previously are ones that I feel are so important for children within the EYFS. It's you and what you believe in and understand as high-quality practice that is the important thing. If that quality is embedded in your practice, then fabulous learning experiences for the children will naturally follow. It's your passion for and commitment to what you have chosen to do that is important, along with interactions from the adults within the space.

DOI: 10.4324/9781003451082-6

Figure 4.1 A photo of a construction space in a school.
Source: Photograph taken by the author

Other learning environments

The experience would be the same if the children were in their home, in a childminder's home, in a setting, in a hospital or in a classroom. Wherever they are, children need to be excited to learn and to engage with their surroundings. They need to be enticed into their learning.

In the context of Early Phonics and the possibilities for the many and varied settings the children might be in, the 'learning environment' could actually be anything. It might just be a basket or container, one room that is packed away at the end of each day, an outdoor space or a large classroom. It really doesn't matter what the size is; it's how it is presented to the child or children and what happens there that is important. We need to think about the learning environment in the context of Early Phonics and how the skills to be developed can and should be threaded robustly through it so it becomes the 'third teacher'.

The learning environment and Early Phonics

It is important to focus on the Early Years learning environment as a means to ensure that children 'stumble across' (metaphorically, not literally) opportunities to practice skills, take ownership of them and develop them in their unique and individual ways. This should be the case whatever you might be teaching, but here we are particularly focusing on the context of Early Phonics.

Early Phonics is generally not a primary focus for most practitioners when creating or 'setting up' learning environments. We know the broadly accepted areas of the provision that need to be in place or the resources to enable children to engage in the activities they afford. This might include a mark-making area of some sort, maths resources, a reading area, construction, music, small world . . . however, within the areas of provision noted, opportunities for Early Phonics can be robustly threaded throughout them. You're honestly missing a trick if you don't consider this.

Planning formats for a learning environment, including Early Phonics

In the appendix, I have included a planning format that you might find useful to ensure that you include authentic Early Phonic opportunities in each learning space of your provision. This is intended as a starting point that will evolve over time. The learning environment planning document will help you to consider each area of your provision, what resources you might place there that could support Early Phonics learning, and some ideas for the adult role or the adult response when sounds are heard or made.

If you work with a team of practitioners, each of you could consider how you could add pertinent Early Phonics opportunities as the children's learning progresses.

To hone these opportunities even further for individual children or small groups, I have included a planning format for this purpose, too.

Both planning formats can be found on our website: *www.therightstartearlyyears.co.uk* so please download, use and/or adapt these to suit you and your setting.

Whilst planning for these experiences, remember that children might have play preferences – spaces they visit more frequently than others. It will be important that you think about how similar experiences can be placed in a variety of spaces to ensure equality of access to the skills for all children.

Why Early Phonic opportunities in the environment are important

Early Phonic learning can very easily be playfully placed into a specific adult-led session, but in addition to this, it really needs to be always available. If you do embed Early Phonics into your provision, you will perhaps 'free up' an adult-led session for something else.

You need to think about each area of learning you are providing and consider exactly what you are offering there that will promote Early Phonics development whether an adult is directly engaging with the children or not.

Use your assessments and knowledge of the children to decide which elements need to be developed. Some potential assessments and responses to these that could be placed in your learning environment are documented in what follows. These activities are for children to 'come across' during their independent learning time. The skill development benefits of these will always be much more effective if they can be shared with the children and their possibilities explored fully with an adult prior to being placed in your environment. The children will then know how to engage with them when they 'come across' them, although, as always, they will also be free to adapt their use as they play!

Assessment considerations

Some potential assessment considerations and possible responses if further development opportunities are needed:

- **Do the children know a good number of nursery rhymes?** Place Nursery rhyme prompts such as puppet-type characters or spoons decorated with nursery rhyme prompts in various places in your provision – reading space, mark-making space and creative space. Encourage adults to spontaneously sing with the children as they play or undertake 'jobs' such as tidying or washing hands.

- **Do the children listen carefully to individual sounds?** All adults should be on a constant alert when close to these children who don't have this skill yet and draw their attention to sounds as they play. If the children are older, prepare methods of noting individual sounds – a chart perhaps, or adding gems to a jar each time a sound is heard that is in the music space. They could then share their findings during a 'plenary' at the end of the session. Create recordings of individual sounds for the children to listen to.

- **Can the children hear sounds in their environments?** Involve them in activities similar to those mentioned previously, but make sure to undertake the activity outdoors as well as inside. The sounds and the children's responses might be very different. Outdoor sounds will be broader in their range and probably a little more surprising and exciting!

- **Can the children discriminate between sounds?** Place two relatively large cardboard boxes containing identical sound makers in a space in your indoor or outdoor environment. This could be in a music space, creative or performance space. Tip the boxes onto their sides, and the children could play a game together, secretly making a sound and seeing if the other person can make the same sound or alternatively make a different sound.

- **Can the children make soft or loud sounds? Do they understand that these sounds are different?** The sound makers for the activity mentioned previously could be used in this activity or your usual provision of musical instruments. Create a dice with different letters, symbols or words to indicate how the sounds should be made.

- **Can they make voice sounds?** This can be undertaken in any learning space, accompaniments to stories, small world characters, animals or transport. Again, use a dice, perhaps placed in your reading space beside the nursery rhyme spoons. Each face of the dice might depict different ways to use the voice when singing a rhyme, such as singing like a snake or like an ogre.

- **Do they understand rhyme and/or alliteration?** Place a die in a learning zone, perhaps in your 'reading space', with simple words/pictures on its faces such as 'cat', 'bag' or 'fish', and as the children roll the die, they need to say a rhyming word. This is an adult-led activity that could be left for the children to access independently and play either alone or with a friend.

These enhancements to your provision are simple, responsive and purposeful. Another piece of advice would be to ensure the resources are moved from time to time to different areas of your provision. Children who access areas less frequently than others will be encouraged to play with them. Others will be reminded of them if they move and are spotted in a different location. Also, when the resource has been accessed well by the children, think about adaptations to extend the learning.

Is your provision purposeful?

Too often, daily phonics sessions are planned as part of Nursery daily routines. Early phonics must be a learning experience for the children but not necessarily as a daily 'session', and it should certainly be planned to incorporate the methods I am sharing in this book. It should be engaging and fun and carefully home in on the children's learning needs.

I am also not suggesting that an 'early phonics area' should be created as a discrete zone of your learning environment. I am suggesting that thought needs to be put into how opportunities to hone and rehearse Early Phonic skills can be considered for each and every area of your learning environment. This will be for each and every child who will play within it. All it takes is a little thought about your learning spaces and which skills your children currently need to hone and use the ideas in this book.

A literacy-rich environment

There are simple ways to create learning opportunities for Early Phonics in your environment. Firstly, something that should always be strived for is a literacy-rich learning environment. The importance of this is highlighted by Sally Neaum (2017): 'Print awareness refers to children's engagement with and developing awareness of print in their environment . . . it is about coming to know what print is, what it is used for and broadly how it works'. This goes hand in hand with all phonic learning, whether early or later.

Use labelling effectively

This is a strategy that is commonly used in Early Years learning environments where the majority of spaces and resources are labelled. I always suggest this is with photos or pictures of the item/s *and* words. I believe it is so important to have both so the children can begin to understand the relationship between the two and ensure that the provision is accessible to all. This way, nobody is disadvantaged by not being able to use their burgeoning phonic ability to read the words – they can read the pictures.

Use 'real' items and products in your environment

I will also mention here the vital importance of having 'real' and authentic items accessible to the children that they might see in other places, including the home and their locality. Display shop names, packaging and food items from whichever culture the children might be from. Having recognisable and familiar items will add to ensuring all children feel equal and as though they belong and are valued. Having rich literacy opportunities surrounding the children will make reading and writing part of a natural process. It will also give adults opportunities to initiate conversations when interacting with the children.

Drawing the children into their learning

In addition to this, the one very simple thing you can do to ensure children are accessing these skills during Child-Initiated Learning (CIL), play, independent time or 'choosing' – whatever you have chosen to call it, is for adults to *draw children's attention* to the learning.

As I have mentioned before, the one significant thread that runs through all learning in the EYFS is the adults 'knowing your children'. Really knowing them. Knowing what makes them tick. Then, you will know exactly what they need to learn next, allowing you to deftly drop that into your interactions with them during their independent play. This is what I will explain as we look at the different learning spaces – I will share some possibilities for learning, particularly through interactions with the children.

How to bring Early Phonics into a high-quality learning environment

It might help us to think about a typical Early Years learning environment. I think this might be a preschool, Nursery or Reception provision. If you are in a different type of provision, you might have an adapted version of this. If you are in a home, it may look a little different again. But the principles are the same. It is very easy, and with a little thought and consideration, it will become a natural part of your daily interactions.

In what follows, I've added some examples of how you could promote Early Phonics in a range of learning spaces in your environment.

(N.B. *The resources are a small number of suggestions for what might typically be in place in your provision, but it is in no way a comprehensive list. For information about your continuous provision you might like to look on our website: www.therightstartearlyyears.co.uk for ideas and inspiration.*)

The ideas noted in what follows are all very much about the adult drawing the children's attention to the sounds that are usually just part of everyday life and that we all take for granted and, as adults, we probably don't normally notice at all. They are all sounds that children can tune into to help them become more alert about hearing sounds in the first place. They will learn to discriminate between sounds in our environment, which will ultimately support their skills in auditory discrimination. All of this will then underpin their phonics learning when it's time. If you draw children's attention to sounds frequently enough, the children will start having ideas of their own about the sounds they hear. Their vocabulary will also expand as they find words to describe the sounds!

Table 4.1 Examples and ideas

Learning Space	Resources	Adult role and responses/verbalised ponderings
Construction	Wooden blocks	• Note a child tapping the bricks – draw their attention to the sounds they are making: 'Oh, what a lovely hollow sound, the brick sounds empty'. Follow this up by tapping different bricks together; do they make different sounds? • If there are some 'beaters' nearby, then use them to make sounds on the bricks. A wooden spoon, perhaps. The different bricks will make different sounds – you could encourage the children to create a xylophone of bricks! • The sound when a large construction falls down!
	'Lego' type bricks	• Listen to and talk about the 'click' when the bricks are joined together and taken apart • Talk about the sound you hear when a specific brick is being searched for in amongst a pile – the clattering of tiny bricks
	'Mobilo' type construction	• Draw the children's attention to the clicking sounds as the bricks and links snap together • Enjoy the clattering sound as the movable sections are flipped. 'Does anything else make a similar sound?'

(Continued)

Table 4.1 (Continued)

Learning Space	Resources	Adult role and responses/verbalised ponderings
Maths space	Sand timers	• See how many times you can sing a nursery rhyme whilst the sand pours through the timer • See who can make a sound with their voice for the longest time/as long as the sand timer
	Dice and number cards	• Suggest the use of instruments if the children are interested in playing with dice. Place a number card by each instrument and play the instrument when the dice rolls that number. This supports subitising well! You could have two people play (PSED link) the instruments at the same time (EAD/music link!). Talk about the sounds. This game could be from an adult-led session, then left for the children to use independently, or you could sit and enjoy the game with the children during CIL, discussing the sounds. You (or they!) could even record their music and share it with others later. If they are doing this, it will further enhance their burgeoning technology skills! • There are several activities in this book linked to dice. Look out for them
	Dice	• If the children show an interest in the dice, you could suggest a game where the dice dictate the amount of sounds that need to be made. For instance, if you suggest hands clapping and a number six on a dice was rolled, then the player has to clap six times! A fantastic blending of maths and early phonics. Talk about the sounds obviously, loud sounds, quiet claps, fast or slow, etc. Let the children choose the next body sound to use!
Mark-making space	Scissors	• Quite simply draw the children's attention to the snapping sound the scissors make as they cut. Do all scissors make the same sound? What sound does the paper make as it is being cut? Does card or tissue paper sound different from the usual A4 paper?

(Continued)

Table 4.1 (Continued)

Learning Space	Resources	Adult role and responses/verbalised ponderings
	Paper, sticky tape, stapler	• Talk about the sound as the paper is ripped rather than cut or the screech of the sticky tape being unravelled! The click and snap of the stapler, the sound of pen lids being removed and the click as they are replaced (always a great skill to learn!). Some squeaky felt-tipped pens are always fun to listen to! Chalk on boards . . . great sounds, tapping and the screech that sets your teeth on edge
Music space	Variety of instruments, both commercial and homemade	• This entire space is a gift to early phonics and children learning to discriminate between sounds! • As the children explore the instruments, give names to the sounds and encourage them to do the same, making them into little rhymes as they play more than one instrument e.g. clitter clatter, snap snap as the castanets then drums are played one after the other . . . • Roll some beads, beans or marbles around inside a tambour and talk about the continuous swooshing sound they make • Tap the bottom of the tambour with beads inside! Great sound • Ponder as the children and/or you make sounds with the instruments. Talk about the ones you like best and why, and invite the children to do the same
	'Junk' modelling equipment such as boxes, tubes, cartons and pasta or beans to fill them. Add joining materials such as sticky tape and string	• Create a space in the music area where the children can make their own musical instruments. Talk about the sounds their instruments make. Shaking instruments are perfect – some empty plastic water bottles with a variety of items to pour inside. Simple and effective to make contrasting sounds

(Continued)

Table **4.1** (Continued)

Learning Space	Resources	Adult role and responses/verbalised ponderings
	'Beaters' – homemade and commercial. A broad variety of paint brushes, small mops and washing-up brushes, chopsticks (use mindfully being aware of the age of the children and teach how to handle properly), feathers, musical 'beaters', reeds and, of course, fingertips!	• Offer the children a broad range of 'beaters' – homemade or commercial –to tap the instruments with and talk about the sounds • Invite the children to tell you the sound they want to make and encourage them to choose the 'beater' they think will help make that sound • You could categorise the sounds, choosing the categories together. They could be used to create sounds to illustrate a story or poem
Create a listening space	Perhaps include something such as a Tonie or tablet where children can be encouraged to listen to and respond to sounds	• The children could listen to some peaceful music they have created • Ponder with the children about the sounds they hear. 'Tell me what you think?' or 'I wonder . . . ?'-type questions

(*Continued*)

Table **4.1** (Continued)

Learning Space	Resources	Adult role and responses/verbalised ponderings
Small world space	Small people, environments for them to live in, trains, cars, dinosaurs, dolls house, farm sets, birds, 'wild animals'/zoo animals . . .	• The animals are all gifts for making voice sounds – all imaginable and more! Loud sounds, quiet sounds, high and low. If you're rural, make the most of opportunities to go out and hear animals or following a visit to a zoo or farm • Birds are around all of us, so sit quietly and listen . . . • All vehicles make sounds, so if you're able, go out into the environment and find out what you can hear. You may be near a road, so find somewhere safe to listen to cars, aircraft might be going overhead or a railway might be nearby, so focus in on those sounds, too • Encourage the children to replicate these sounds as they play with the small world resources: 'I wonder what sound the elephant might make?' – make it up if you haven't heard one yet, and check later! Dinosaurs can definitely be made up! • If the children are creating a narrative as they play, suggest that they record the story and add sound effects to it • Sing nursery rhymes such as 'Old MacDonald' if the children are playing with farm animals and encourage them to join in
Painting space	Music source plus painting resources of any kind	• Whilst the children are engaging in their painting, play some emotive music that will inspire their painting. Talk with them about the music as they work – what does it sound like, remind them of, make them think of or feel? • Talk about the sound of the paint or the sound the brush makes • If using rollers with paint, talk about the squelching sounds • Using large wallpaper, can the children draw the sounds using large scale motor movements? E.g. if it's a sharp sound, they might draw jagged shapes; if it's a long sound, they may draw a long line . . .

(Continued)

Table 4.1 (Continued)

Learning Space	Resources	Adult role and responses/verbalised ponderings
Role play space	Many and varied depending on the context	• Sounds that are made during the play situation – encourage the children to make vocal sounds to accompany their play • I always used a 'music' session to explore the instruments, then add them to the role play space to create atmospheric sound effects e.g. we worked with instruments to find those which sounded like the sea, then placed them in the Pirate Ship role play space. The music session encouraged 'tuning into' sounds, then the exploration afterwards developed skills further
	Home corner	• Join the play and talk about the sounds they might hear in the home. Do they have the same sounds at home or different ones? A washing machine, a kettle, a microwave?
	Hairdressers	• Talk to the children about the sounds of the scissors and try to make these as voice sounds. Consider also the sound of the hairdryer or the water for washing hair
	General	• Encourage the children to sing songs or recite rhymes they are familiar with that are linked to the role play space e.g. 'The Wheels on the Bus' for a bus role play space • Look at books that have been placed in the role play space Can you add sound effects as you share the story or information?
Fine motor space	Varied to support fine motor skill development	• Work alongside the children, engaging them in conversation. When a sound is made, draw their attention to it, such as the pinging of a rubber band when stretched, the scuttling sound of beads or beans in a dish, the clicking of tweezers, the gorgeous squelchy sounds of clay – especially when wet!, nuts and bolts tinkling and squeaking, the rubbing of pipe cleaners being pulled through a sieve . . . so many sounds to draw the children's attention to

(Continued)

Table 4.1 (Continued)

Learning Space	Resources	Adult role and responses/verbalised ponderings
Water space (indoor and/ or outdoor)	A water tray of any size, a range of resources. Create a water wall outside	• Talk to the children about the sounds they make as they play. Offer the differing language to describe the sounds – thus expanding their vocabulary e.g. 'I love the splooshing sound the water makes when you swirl it around – it reminds me of . . .' • Offering the children metal containers to play with will create a whole range of new sounds. Remind them of the game 'Bath time taps' (see 'activities) to explore the sounds • If the children are filling 'capacity' jugs or containers, encourage them to tap them to investigate the sounds they make.
	Resources to help move water from one place to another	• Support the children as they work out how to move water from one place to another and invite the children to hear and describe the sounds as the water moves • See if the children are able to change the sounds of the moving water and talk about which sound is loudest
Sand space (indoor and/ or outdoor)	Wet and dry sand with a range of high-quality resources	• Find a quiet moment to encourage the children to listen to the sounds of the sand • Investigate together the different sounds of wet and dry sand. The sound of a spade pushing its way through wet sand . . . can they recreate that sound with their voices? • Talk about the sound of larger vehicles with their wheels pressing the sand • Join the children in their play and model slowly dropping dry sand onto different surfaces e.g. the bottom of a bucket, into a metal container. See if you/they can change the sound
Outdoor space	A range of 'beaters' Logs	• Join the children in their play if they are by some logs. Investigate the sounds as you tap different lengths of log. I once had some children independently create a xylophone out of a series of logs placed alongside each other, played with wooden spoons! • Provide 'beaters' and encourage the children to simply tap all manner of items when outside. Talk with them about the different sounds they make!

(Continued)

Table **4.1** (Continued)

Learning Space	Resources	Adult role and responses/verbalised ponderings
	Bird watching space	• Make bird feeders with the children and hang them in the bird watching space, then encourage the children to watch for birds (link to Understanding the World). Listen out for the sounds of birds and try to mimic them. Apps are available to help identify bird calls
	Outdoor music space	• Create a sound wall as in the indoor music space with the children. Talk about the different sounds they can make • In a 'performance' space, add resources that support making sound effects for a familiar story, rhyme or song for the children to use and encourage/support their use
EAD ('creative') space	All junk modelling items – boxes, packaging, bottles . . .	• Whilst you are engaging with the child as they play in the creative space, comment on the sounds of the items they are working with e.g. pick up a box and tap on it – 'What does it sound like: low, high, hollow?' Then, compare it to another box. All of this in the manner of a chatty conversation, rather than intense questioning! • As in the mark-making space – draw their attention to the sounds of their tools, the scissors cutting, the tape being unravelled or sliced by the dispenser . . .
	Bottles, small items such as lentils, rice or pasta	• Model how to make sound-makers with the children – adding small items of different sorts to the bottles and moving them in different ways to create sounds
	Sound wall	• Make a sound or music wall or portable board with the children using all manner of things that make sounds from crinkly paper and corrugated cardboard or pots and pans, lids, whisks and baking tins
Woodwork space	**Risk-assessed tools and equipment –** saws, hammers, nails, screws, sandpaper, wrench, vice . . .	• Talk about the sounds of the resources – the pins/screws/nails as they are moved in a pot or container, the sounds of the hammers and saws as they are used • Encourage the children to think about the sounds they can make with the resources – cork, soft wood and other loose parts • Perhaps 'sound-makers' could be designed and made in the woodwork space!

(Continued)

Table 4.1 (Continued)

Learning Space	Resources	Adult role and responses/verbalised ponderings
Wellbeing space	A quiet space outside	• Work with the children to create some beautiful, gentle sound-makers for this space, such as chimes with shells, discs or bamboo. Talk about the sounds and how they make the children feel • Are the sounds different in the wind or rain?
Malleable space	Dough, made by the children, homemade or commercial. A range of utensils such as rolling pins, items to press into the dough, pestle and mortar . . .	• Encourage the children to join in with songs you sing as they play that are linked to what they are making e.g. 'Pat-a-cake', 'Happy Birthday' • Say the names of the utensils the children are using and try to create rhyming words such as mortar/water, roller/stroller
	Homemade dough	• Encourage the children to talk about the sounds created as the dough is being made, mixing up the ingredients and the luscious sound as liquid is added!

An accessible approach

The ideas I have shared for ensuring Early Phonics is accessible across a learning environment will mean that children are naturally exploring and honing these early reading skills in every learning space you have created. This will ensure the children have depth and breadth when learning these Early Phonic skills as they are mastered across the three categories of Sounds Around, Sounds We Make and Sounds with Words.

A calm environment

Clearly, a calm learning environment is going to support good listening. In the previous table, I talked about the need for a quiet space, a space within a busier learning environment that is away from the main hustle and bustle for listening. There are a number of reasons for creating this space, but for Early Phonics, this space is necessary when working with children who need extra support to refine their listening skills. It is a place where distractions are limited and individual sounds can be clearly heard.

However, adults also need to think about the general ambience of the space where children are learning, whatever type of setting they might be in. The emotional environment is as important as the sensory nature of the space. With Early Phonics, the children need to feel calm and secure to be able to really focus on the sounds we want them to hear.

Points to peruse and ponder . . .

- What are the key elements of early phonics that you think your child/children need to focus on?

- Have you got to know your children well, and have you created opportunities in the learning environment that will motivate and excite children to want to learn e.g. are children interested in dinosaurs, painting, etc.? Can you provide early phonics opportunities linked to these?

- Which learning spaces do you have in your provision, and what Early Phonics learning could you add to them?

- Once your environment is complete, evaluate it again, either now or over time, to make sure it includes plenty of early phonics opportunities. You need to remember to be responsive to your children's evolving learning needs

- Are you and all other adults confident you can support Early Phonics in each of these spaces?

- Use the template provided to start adding your resources and adult support suggestions

- Consider some conversation starters for each learning space that would support Early Phonics. If you work with others, generate these as a team so everyone feels invested in the process

- How are you creating literacy-rich learning environments?

References

Neaum, Sally. 2017. *What Comes Before Phonics?* London: Sage.
Pound, Linda. 2007. *How Children Learn.* London: Step Forward Publishing.

Part Two

Early Phonics activities

5 Introduction to Part Two

In this chapter

This chapter is to explain how the activities in the following three chapters are to be used. The information includes:

- How the three groups of activities have been organised and why this is so

- How to use the activities

- An important reminder that the activities are not designed to be worked through in order from start to finish and why it is important that they are not

The Early Phonics activities

The activities shared in the following three chapters have been created to provide adults with a useful resource to support their teaching of Early Phonics to young children. The activities are to support children across the EYFS age range, from those approaching 12 months to those at the end of the Key Stage who are 5+ years. I have used some with children from nearly three months old! The activities can also be used with children who are older, working in Key Stage One, and are even adaptable for children older than this, if needed.

The skills

The activities have been placed into three categories that categorise them according to the set of skills they have been created to develop. They are:

Sounds Around
Sounds We Make
Sounds With Words

DOI: 10.4324/9781003451082-8

Sounds Around involves all the sounds we may hear in our environments, both indoors and outside. The activities encourage children to listen carefully to what is happening around them, from playing in the bath (or water tray) to focusing on sounds made by wooden objects to games that can be played in a shop, whether real or role play. The emphasis is that sounds come in many guises, are all around us and are there for us to listen to!

Sounds We Make includes a range of activities that can be made by us. In the activities for the youngest children, the sounds might be made by an adult, but the vast majority are sounds to be made by the children. Children might be invited to use different 'beaters' to create sounds or use their voices to create sounds.

Sounds With Words is very much about singing songs and nursery rhymes, and some activities also involve books, with or without text. As always, many of the activities are suitable for undertaking indoors or outside. Rhyme, alliteration and early aural phoneme activities are explored, along with ways to change how we sing by making things faster or slower!

How to use the activities

The activities can be used as a general resource to add an Early Phonics element to your daily routine at any time during your session.

- They can be used to provide a learning activity for an adult-led session, where the adult leads the learning

- Following an adult-led session, they can then be left for the children to access independently during their child-initiated learning time

- They can be used to robustly support assessments that have been made of the children's developing skills in Early Phonics, finely tuning activities to the children's learning needs

- When the adult identifies the skills the children need to practice or develop, the chapter titles will make finding the focused activities to support the learning a simple process. For example, if you realise the children know few nursery rhymes, then you might focus firstly on the section 'Sounds with Words'

- In addition to the three chapter categories, the activities also have notes on how long it is expected that each activity might take to complete. This guide is intended to help adults make the best use of the time they have available

- It is expected that the activities will be repeated over time. Children will love the familiarity of a game. If you feel the children are ready to change or develop the activity slightly to further their skills, each one has noted ways in which you might change the game under the heading 'Additional Ideas'

■ With each activity, there is an explanation about 'why' the skills the activity will support are important. This is to ensure that the adult supporting the activity will be able to focus on the potential learning. It will support them in thinking of questions to ask the children as the activity progresses to probe their thinking and reasoning

■ Additionally, there is a section with the heading 'Making other connections'. This will help the adult to quickly see what other areas of learning are being supported by the activity. Again, this will help the adult to focus on potential learning opportunities and help the children to make connections in their learning

An important note

I would like to reassure you that the activities are in no way meant to be a list that is worked through from start to finish. They have been created for you to 'dip into' as you wish or need. It is important that the activities are responsive to the learning needs and assessments of the children. The whole principle of *The Right Start to Phonics* is that the activities are playful and fun, both for children and adults, thus having a positive impact on learning.

6 Sounds Around

In this chapter

This chapter provides adults with a variety of activities to be shared with children that will support and encourage them to listen carefully to sounds they might hear around them both indoors and outside.

Sounds Around activities

DOI: 10.4324/9781003451082-9

Bathtime Taps!

No better place to have phonic fun than in the bath! This is a gentle, calming activity that can be done just as well in a water tray.

What you'll need:

- A selection of metal containers such as biscuit or cake tins, metal cooking or serving pots, other small tins, metal jugs

- A metal teaspoon or larger spoon

Figure 6.1 A photograph of a bath with metal objects in it.
Source: Photograph taken by the author

Step by step:

- Place one of your metal containers in the bath or water tray and make sure it is floating. Once it is floating, add a little water to it and tap it with your teaspoon

- Listen to the sound it makes as you 'chime' the metal and the water moves within the container

- Encourage your child/ren to gently tap the pot and listen to the sound it makes

- Add other pots to the water and repeat the process

- Talk about the sounds you hear; describe the sounds

Additional ideas:

- Try doing the activity with other containers. Does it work as well with plastic or wood? Talk about the differences in sound with the other materials

Why?

This is a gentle activity to be undertaken in a quiet space. Tuning into the quieter, calm sounds is very important as these are the sounds that are often overlooked in our busy lives. If you are in a busy learning environment, try taking a large bucket of water to a quieter space, indoors or outside, to make the most of a quiet opportunity for listening.

Making other connections

This activity will help develop skills in **Personal, Social and Emotional Development.** The calm and gentle sounds will encourage mindfulness and peace, supporting well-being and self-regulation. **Literacy** skills, particularly in the area of 'listening', will be supported by this activity. The hustle and bustle of daily life makes focused listening a challenge. This activity will also have a positive impact on **EAD** with the 'musical' nature of the sounds heard.

Sound Around

Dapper Tappers

This simple game will give your child or children a great reason to tap!

What you'll need:

■ A range of 'beaters' that are safe for children to play with such as: wooden and metal spoons, jug mops, washing up brushes, scrubbing brushes, paint brushes of differing sizes, chopsticks (supervised according to age), pencils, makeup brushes, sticks, plastic and/or metal whisk . . .

■ A box and bucket

■ A bag or box to hold and conceal the 'beaters'

Figure 6.2 A photograph of a shoebox with a spatula, paintbrush, spoon, chopsticks etc and a bucket.
Source: Photograph taken by the author

Step by step:

■ Find somewhere comfortable to sit with your child or children

■ Introduce the 'beaters' one at a time to your child or children. Talk about what each one is, naming it and talking about its usual purpose

■ Suggest you are going to see if you can make the 'beater' make a sound. Start tapping it either on your box or your bucket

Sounds Around

- Talk about the sound it makes, then try tapping it on a different surface (bucket or box) and talk about how the sound is changing

- Take another 'beater' out of your bag or box and go through the same process with it

- Talk about/ask about how the sounds are different

Additional ideas:

- You could start this activity with just one or two beaters, then build up the selection

- Add a different surface to tap – you could end up with a homemade drum kit! Add a saucepan, a plastic container, some bubble wrap or a wooden box

- Always remember to draw your child's attention to the sound being made

- This activity will be great to play either inside or outdoors

- Why not use the sounds you create to accompany a song or nursery rhyme?

- Try to find two or more sounds that sound really similar or really different and sort them into groups

Why?

Using everyday items to make sounds will encourage your child to undertake this activity at other times and tune in to the sounds being made.

Making other connections

There will be a connection here with **Understanding the World** as the children's attention is drawn to the everyday items being used and their 'normal' use is discussed. Adding a song to the play will reinforce the musical element in **Expressive Arts and Design.** If you categorise the 'beaters' into sets of the sound they make, you will be adding a **Mathematical** dimension to the play!

Walk-a-Sound

You could make sure you do this activity during each changing season or whenever you visit somewhere special, such as a forest or a beach.

What you'll need:

■ You and a child or children together in an outdoor environment

Figure 6.3 A photo of an adult and child's feet walking outside.
Source: Photograph taken by the author

Step by step:

■ As you walk outside with your child or children, invite them to focus on the sounds their feet are making

■ See how you can make the sounds louder or more noticeable as you walk e.g. stamping, or dragging your feet

■ If you are able, walk on different surfaces e.g. if you are on a path

- Listen to the sound of your feet on the concrete or paving slabs, then walk on the grass

- How does the sound change?

- Does it change again if you change the way you are walking?

- As you continue on your walk, see how the sounds change

  - Walk through fallen leaves

  - Walk in puddles

  - Walk on soil or grass

  - Walk on sand or a pebbly beach

- All the time you are walking, talk about the distinctive sounds you are making and find words to describe the sounds

Additional ideas:

- Make a recording of the sounds you make to listen to later and to compare in another season

- See if you can recreate the different sounds once you are home/back in your setting

- Make a 'sound path' outside your home or setting using trays or boxes containing different things e.g. pebbles, slate fragments, moss or bark. Try walking on your 'sound path' with different footwear to see if the sounds change

Why?

This is another everyday activity that we can use to develop auditory awareness in small children. If you recreate your own 'sound path' afterwards, this will really focus children's attention and remind them of the sounds they heard.

Making other connections

Physical Development will be enhanced by taking the children for a healthy walk. **Understanding the World** will be supported by children's attention being focused on the world around them and taking notice of what is beneath their feet.

Softly Softly Sounds

This activity will help children to focus specifically on one type of sound.

What you'll need:

■ The space you are in – just the things around you, wherever you are

■ For the additional activity, a range of 'soft beaters' – brushes, thin items such as straws and chopsticks, feathers and fingertips!

Figure 6.4 A photo of a collection of feathers, chopsticks, straws and fingertips.
Source: Photograph taken by the author

Step by step:

■ Sit with your child or group of children. Say that you are going to think about sounds, but today, you are going to find the quietest, softest sounds you can!

- Model how to tap very gently on a surface near you, rub two fabrics together or tap on your knees and ask if they can hear the really quiet sound. Ask if they can copy your really quiet sound

- Invite them to look around and see what are the quietest sounds they can make. Share these with each other and talk about the sounds. Find ways to describe them. Are they scratchy, rustling, swishy?

- When they have explored with their hands and fingers, ask if they could use any other body parts to make really quiet sounds. Talk about any sounds they make and find which body part makes the softest sound e.g. knee, foot, elbow?

Additional ideas:

- Extend the activity by introducing the gentle 'beaters' to gently tap items in your space. Ask the children if these are quieter or louder than your fingers and hands

- The activity can take place both indoors or outside

Why?

With this activity, you will be encouraging your children to really listen carefully to the sounds they can hear. If you have played the Metal Sounds game, compare the sounds that they have made in the two activities, or if not, play the Metal Sounds game soon after playing this game. It's a good strategy to encourage the children to compare and see the differences between the sounds they have made.

Making other connections

You will be engaging the children in many elements of **Communication and Language** with this activity, sharing new language with the items being played and in the descriptions and conversations had as they move around. The children will be active, so they will be developing their **Physical** skills. Take the activity outside for even more physicality!

Room Sounds

This will really help children to focus in on those everyday sounds that so often just pass us by.

What you'll need:

■ You and a child or children together as you move around your space

Figure 6.5 A photo of a bathroom.
Source: Photograph taken by the author

Step by step:

■ As you move around your space, perhaps with a child at home or around your setting as you do chores or for whatever reason, encourage focused listening

■ For example, draw your child's attention to the different sounds your feet make on floor surfaces. Is there a difference between rooms or spaces? Do you have to tap your feet to hear a sound? How are the sounds different?

Sounds Around

- Other sounds you can draw your child's attention to are taps and running water, toilets flushing, household appliances – washing machine, tumble dryer, dishwasher, vacuum cleaner, hair dryer or fan, the sound of surfaces being sprayed, windows opening or closing, doorbells, doors opening or closing, keyboards being tapped, electronic devices, printers, phones ringing, chairs moving, food preparation sounds – chopping, grating, mixing . . .

- There are so many sounds that we just ignore because they happen daily. But take the time to have 'listening ears' on some days. You might take an hour, a morning, a day or a week. Just be sure to notice everyday sounds in your home or setting

- Encourage the children to begin describing the sounds. What is the quality (timbre) of the sound? Is it fast or slow, smooth or jerky? What words can the children come up with to describe these sounds?

Additional ideas:

- You could make a pictorial or photographic list of the sounds you hear. You could even categorise these into the rooms where they are heard. Draw a picture of your house or setting. Which room is the noisiest or has the most sounds?

Why?

This is one of the fundamental themes of *The Right Start to Phonics* – *tuning in to sounds*. Children are so accustomed, probably from before birth, to the sounds around them that they become 'wallpaper', so are not really listened to. This activity will draw children's attention to sounds and encourage them to discriminate between them.

Making other connections

With this activity, children are encouraged to really pay attention to the sounds around them and what is making them, which will support learning in **Understanding the World.** Describing the sounds will support their development in **Literacy** by building vocabulary and **Expressive Arts and Design** with the musical element of 'timbre'. If you undertake the extension activity, children will be sorting and categorising the sounds, too, whichwill add a **Mathematics** dimension to the activity.

Remember Remember

This is an activity that can be undertaken anywhere at any time!

What you'll need:

■ Just you and your child or children

Figure 6.6 A photo of a man talking to a child outside.
Source: Photograph taken by the author

Step by step:

■ As you go about your daily life or routines, talking to your child or children as you work, from time to time, ask them to help you to remember things

■ Say things such as 'I mustn't forget to buy some oranges when we go shopping, do you think you could help me to remember them please?' or 'We must not forget to take the chalk outside with us when we go. Do you think you can help me to remember that please?'

- Then later on, when you go shopping or go outside, pretend you have forgotten what it was you asked them to remember . . . 'Oh goodness me, I've forgotten what we needed to buy at the shop, can you remember?' or 'What was it we needed to take outside, I've completely forgotten, can you remember?' making the child feel important as they have remembered and you, as the adult didn't!

Additional ideas:

- Start with one thing and then add one more, and one more again over time, so the list might have two or three items

Why?

Holding things in your memory is one of the important executive functions that children need to develop. This is especially vital for children who are going to learn to use the phonic approach to read and write. They will need to hold the sounds in their head in order to use them to blend them to read and segment them to write.

Making other connections

The connections to other areas of learning with this activity are with **Personal, Social and Emotional Development** and a child's sense of self. It is important that a child feels involved in daily routines and tasks and is made to feel valuable. **Communication and Language** will be supported with the development of both listening, speaking and taking part in a conversation. **Understanding the World** will develop as children make connections in their environment.

Floor Drop

It might be fun to introduce this activity after you and your child or children notice the noise when something is accidentally dropped on the floor. If your child is small, they could sit on a chair or in a highchair for this activity.

What you'll need:

■ You and a child or children in your home or setting

■ A selection of objects that will not break when dropped on the floor – see ideas that follow

Figure 6.7 A photo of a spatula, a lemon squeezer, a teaspoon and a tiny grater on a wooden floor.
Source: Photograph taken by the author

Step by step:

■ Gather together a selection of items that will not break (or cause damage) when dropped on the floor e.g. a dessert spoon, a teaspoon, a wooden spoon, a whisk (metal or plastic), a plastic container, a cardboard box, a grater, a cork, a pen or

Sounds Around

pencil, a rubber, a plastic bowl, a birthday card, a duster, a brush, a feather, a cotton wool ball, a shoe, a plastic cup or beaker, a peg (wooden and/or plastic), a coaster, a baking sheet, a table mat . . .

- Place these items in a box or bag

- Take one item out of your bag or box and drop it on the floor – show surprise at the sound it makes. Pick it up and encourage your child to do the same as you and drop it on the floor!

- If your child is old enough to understand, drop an item on the floor behind them and see if they can guess which item you dropped. You could take turns in this version of the game

- Talk about the sounds the items make as they drop on the floor e.g. bang, clatter, splat, ting . . .

- Move to a room with a different floor surface and play the game there and bring your child's attention to the different sounds the items make when they're dropped

Additional ideas:

- You could make a list of the sounds the objects make, modelling writing for your child or children

Why?

Small children often like to drop things on the floor when learning about 'cause and effect' amongst other things. Adults also drop things, too, usually accidentally! Take time to acknowledge this by focusing on the sounds made. Lovely loud clatters and crashes – it's fun to make really loud sounds. Children can be encouraged to really focus and listen when guessing what made that sound.

Making other connections

Physical Development could be enhanced as children pick up and release items with their hands to drop them on the floor. **Literacy** skills could be supported with the 'additional idea' as the adult models the writing of a list and with the naming of the sounds the dropped items make, building the children's descriptive vocabulary.

Bucket Splash

A simple activity that makes the most of the sound of deep water in a bucket.
(N.B. This activity needs to be supervised by an adult, as the expectation is for the bucket to be filled with water.)

What you'll need:

■ Two (or three) clean household-type buckets filled close to the top with clean water

■ A selection of 'waterproof' items to be dropped into the bucket of water

Figure 6.8 A photo of a child dropping a pebble into
a bucket of water with the resulting splash visible.
Source: Photograph taken by the author

Step by step:

■ Gather the items that you will drop into the water. This can be done prior to starting the activity or can be done with your child or children e.g. pebbles, seeds, pine cones, spoons, brushes, twigs, conkers, plastic pots or bottles, coins, keys . . .

■ *This activity would be best undertaken outdoors, but if you do it inside, place the buckets on large groundsheets, tarpaulins or perhaps in a large builder's tray in case of spillages. Be mindful of slippery floors!*

■ Work with your child or children to fill the bucket almost to the rim with clean water

- Select something heavy from your items e.g. a pebble, and drop it into the bucket of water from a reasonable height to ensure it makes a great sound. Talk to the children about the sound

- Invite your child or children to do the same. At first, they can do it with the same item you used. Talk again about the sounds made

- Invite your child or children to select another item and listen together as it is dropped into the bucket of water

- It will be interesting to discuss how to make great sounds; for instance, if a teaspoon is dropped in by the handle first, it will make a little sound, but sideways will be much more satisfying!

- Use the extra buckets for more sploshing fun, where the children explore independently to see what sounds they can make

Additional ideas:

- Invite the children to place the items in sets of good sounds and not-so-good sounds according to their preference

- Try doing the activity with other containers. Does it work as well with plastic or wood? Talk about the differences in sound with the other materials

Why?

Children will love the practical (and somewhat messy) nature of this activity. Listening carefully to the sounds and noticing how they are different will support auditory skill development as well as basic scientific analysis!

Making other connections

There are links to **Understanding the World,** especially if the children help you to gather the items, working out the properties to ensure they will be 'waterproof'. Pondering why some items make more sound than others will engage the children in scientific investigations and use some of the characteristics of effective learning – problem solving and critical thinking. If you decide to place the items into sets, then **Mathematical** skills will be honed.

Tap Tap Tappers

This activity is an extension of Dapper Tappers!

What you'll need:

■ A range of 'beaters' that are safe for children to play with, such as wooden and metal spoons, jug mops, washing up brushes, scrubbing brushes, paint brushes of differing sizes, chopsticks (supervised according to age), pencils, makeup brushes, sticks, plastic and/or metal whisk . . .

■ The environment around you

■ A bag or box to hold and conceal the 'beaters'

Figure **6.9** A photo of three kitchen utensils beside a chair leg on a wooden floor.
Source: Photograph taken by the author

Step by step:

■ Find a space to work in with your child or children. This can be either indoors or outside

■ Model to your children how to select a beater (talk about what you have chosen, discuss its 'normal use') and then find something close to you to tap e.g. a chair, table, the floor, the ground outside. Focus on the sound it makes and try to find words to describe the sound

■ Encourage your child or children to select a 'beater' each and look for something close by to tap. Tap the same thing together and talk about the different sounds made

■ Invite the children to tap something else and discuss the sounds made

■ Your child or children can then move freely around your space, tapping different things and talking about the sounds made

■ When they have used their 'beater' to tap several different things, ask if they would like to choose a different 'beater'. They could swap with a friend or choose something new from your selection

Additional ideas:

■ See if your child or children are able to change the sound they have made. Can they make it quieter or louder?

■ Ask them to recreate their favourite sound and tap along to accompany a song

Why?

Using everyday items to make sounds will encourage your child to undertake this activity at other times and tune in to the sounds being made. It will also focus their sense of hearing on the sounds they can make and how they can change them.

Making other connections

Elements of **Personal, Social and Emotional Development** will be explored with the social nature of the game and when the 'rules' are adhered to. Skills in **Communication and Language** will develop as they listen to you and talk to you/each other and generate descriptive words for the sounds. **Understanding the World and Expressive Arts and Design** will be developed through them exploring their environment and talking about the sounds made.

Magic Music

A gentle listening game that could be played equally well both indoors and outside!

What you'll need:

■ Two sets of matching simple musical instruments (enough for as many children as you have playing the game) e.g. two tambourines, two maracas, two castanets, two triangles, two jingle bells, two guiros, two wood blocks . . . (would be enough for seven children to play).

■ A large pillowcase or large drawstring-type bag

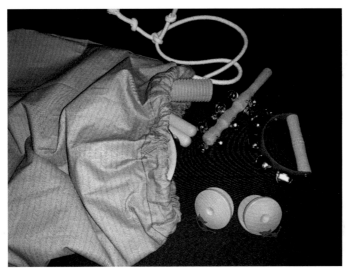

Figure 6.10 A photo of a drawstring bag and some wooden musical instruments.
Source: Photograph taken by the author

Step by step:

■ Find a suitably quiet space for this game, either indoors or outside

■ Show the instruments to the children, saying the instruments' correct names and playing them to demonstrate their sounds

■ When you have done this, place one of each pair of instruments on the floor/space in front of you and place the other one in your pillowcase or bag

■ Invite the children one at a time to choose one of the instruments that are on the floor and place it right in front of them (but then don't touch it!). If you are playing

Sounds Around

with just one or two children, either place all of the 'second' instruments in front of one child or divide them equally between the two

■ Tell the children that you are going to make a 'magic sound' inside your pillowcase or bag, and they will have to listen very carefully. If they think that the sound you are making matches the instrument that they have in front of them, they need to play their instrument!

■ As they start to play their instrument, you slowly reveal the one you are secretly playing. If they match, you can all celebrate! If they don't, talk about the sound carefully and see if another instrument would be a better match

■ Place your instrument back in your bag, and the game continues as you play another instrument

Additional ideas:

■ You could invite one of the children to be the magical music-maker and secretly play a sound for the others to listen to and match

■ Instead of musical instruments, you could use objects from your environment, such as keys, pens, tin foil, etc.

Why?

Here, you will be really helping the children focus on listening carefully to the sounds they are hearing. They will naturally, and probably instinctively, classify them as metallic, wooden or multiple sounds (as with the seeds in maracas).

Making other connections

The children will be fine-tuning their listening skills, so they will be developing aspects of **Communication and Language** with this activity and also **Personal Social and Emotional** skills with the turn-taking and sharing the mutual enjoyment of the game and playing the instruments. There are added links with the musical aspect of **Expressive Arts and Design.**

Wooden Sounds

This activity will help children to focus specifically on one type of sound.

What you'll need:

- An array of wooden objects to make sounds with e.g. cooking utensils, pots, bowls, (non-precious) ornaments and any other small wooden items

- A box or bag in which to place the objects noted previously

Figure 6.11 A photo of a collection of wooden objects, including a spoon, three bowls, a toast rack, a slice of a tree trunk, a box, a gavel and a tray.
Source: Photograph taken by the author

Step by step:

- Gather your child or children together and share the wooden objects you have in your box

- Engage the children in a discussion as you share the objects with them e.g. do they know what these things are? Have they seen any of them before? Can they imagine what they might be used for?

- Advise the children of any objects they might need to be careful with

- Pick up an object and flick it with your finger. Ask the children if they can hear a sound. Talk about the sound you have made

- Repeat this process with another object and continue until all of the objects have been flicked. Then, invite the children to do the same and compare the sounds made

Additional ideas:

- Extend the activity by introducing 'beaters' to gently tap the wooden objects

- Invite the children to explore their environment, finding and making sounds with any wooden furniture they can find. Move around with the children as they explore. Talk about the sounds they make – are they the same or different from the sounds they made on the small objects

Why?

Again, you will be encouraging your children to really listen carefully to the sounds they can hear. If you have played the Metal Sounds game, compare the sounds that they have made in the two activities, or if not, play the Metal Sounds game soon after playing this game. It's a good strategy to encourage the children to compare and see the differences between the sounds they have made.

Making other connections

You will be engaging the children in a great deal of elements of **Communication and Language** with this activity, sharing new language with the objects being played and in the descriptions and conversations they had as they moved around. The children will be active, so they will be developing their **Physical** skills. Take the activity outside for even more physicality!

I Spy Rhymes

This activity will engage the children in a very familiar family game but with an early phonics twist!

What you'll need:

■ You will just need yourselves and the environment you are in!

Figure **6.12** A photo of a large peg and a brown egg.
Source: Photograph taken by the author

Step by step:

■ Tell your child or children that you are going to play a game. If they know the game of 'I Spy', you can tell them that it will be a bit the same but also a bit different! If they are unsure of the game, you will need to explain a little more

■ The important thing is to really think hard about the rhymes. If your child or children are not very experienced with rhymes, you might need to practice, sing some nursery rhymes or play some of the other rhyming games to tune them into rhyming words

- You will start the game by saying,

- 'I spy, with my little eye, something that rhymes with . . .' and finish with something that rhymes with something you can see! If you can see a mug, you could say '. . . rhymes with PUG or BUG'. If you can see a door, you could say 'FLOOR' or 'POOR' or if you see a peg, you could say 'EGG'

- Once the object has been accurately guessed, it is the next person's turn

- You can keep going with this game for as long as your child or children remain focused and are having fun!

Additional ideas:

- The important thing is that those playing the game really understand rhymes, so play games such as Circular Rhymes first to 'tune them in'

- It is equally important that they know how to play the usual game of 'I Spy', so perhaps play this first, too!

Why?

Rhyme is an important early reading skill for a child to understand. It will tune them in to sounds and give them some support and understanding of how words 'work' when they begin to read and write independently.

Making other connections

Personal, Social and Emotional Development will be enhanced through this lovely, calm social activity. Any number of people can play this game. **Communication and Language** will be nourished with the naming of things in your environment, broadening vocabulary.

The Shopping Game

This is a favourite children's game, but it is played here with an early phonics twist!

What you'll need:

- Yourself and the children you are with

- For younger children, you might like to gather together some items that start with the same sound that could be used as prompts e.g. candle, cup, cat, cake, crisps, coffee . . . or mug, mat, map, maple syrup, marbles . . .

Figure 6.13 A photo of a small shopping basket with a clock, carrot, courgette, cucumber, cup, coaster, cat, candle, key and a clip.
Source: Photograph taken by the author

Step by step:

- Sit somewhere comfortable with your child or children and explain the game. If you are using the prompts, place them on the floor or on a table in front of you so they can be seen. Talk about the items and establish that they all begin with the same sound

- Explain how the game will work. You will take the first turn and say, 'I went to the shop and I saw/bought a . . . cup'. The next person then says, 'I went to the shop and I saw (something also beginning with the sound 'c') a cat', then the next person says, 'I went to the shop and I saw a . . . candle'

■ For older children or those who are able, the list could be expanded so the first person says, 'I saw a cup' and the next person has to say, 'I saw a cup and a cat', then the next person has to say 'I saw a cup and a cat and a candle' . . . and so on. See how far you can get!

■ The game ends when somebody cannot think of another item beginning with that letter. You could then, of course, continue the game with another sound!

Additional ideas:

■ You could choose the initial letter of the name of the child you are playing with – next time, choose another person if you are working with a small group.

Why?

This game will really focus the children on the initial sounds of the words they are saying themselves and listening carefully to those said by others. This focus on the initial sounds will help them when they come to blend sounds aurally to hear words and when they begin to read independently.

Making other connections

Personal, Social and Emotional Development will be supported by the warm, social aspect of this game. **Communication and Language** and **Literacy** will be honed through the discussion and thinking of all the words they know that begin with the same initial sound and others that they are learning from you and their friends.

Sounds All Around Us

You could enjoy this activity during each changing season or whenever you visit somewhere unusual such as a forest or a beach, or just in a car park or on a bus or train.

What you'll need:

■ You and a child or children together in an outdoor environment

Figure 6.14 A photo of clouds.
Source: Photograph taken by the author

Step by step:

■ Take your child or children for a walk outdoors. Take some time to sit somewhere quietly on a bench, on a low wall or on the grass and focus on the moment by looking up at the clouds passing by

■ Once you are calm and settled, encourage your child or children to listen really carefully to the sounds that you can hear around you

Sounds Around

- You could take it in turns to quietly say the name of a sound that you hear e.g. birds singing, a car horn, the wind in the trees, a passing helicopter, the bus doors . . .

Additional ideas:

- When your child is playing in a different situation e.g. role play train, remind them of the sounds they heard when you were on a real train and try to replicate them
- If your child is not able to spend time outside in these situations, make or find a recording of the places to play back to your child and play the game electronically!

Why?

This activity will really encourage your child to focus on sounds when there might be a lot of other distractions. This will clarify their hearing and fine-tune their auditory discrimination. So much sound in our daily lives becomes 'wallpaper' and is ignored. This will support your child to be 'present' with their hearing.

Making other connections

Understanding the World will be supported through children taking notice of their surroundings and being aware of what is going on around them. For those children who do not visit other environments, this will bolster their 'cultural capital', giving them experiences they might not otherwise have had.

Techno Sound Play

Tuning into everyday sounds in our environment.

What you'll need:

■ Find some objects that are 'electronic' or use electricity to make them work e.g. a technological device such as Alexa, a vacuum cleaner, a mobile phone, an electronic toy, a remote-controlled toy

Always ensure that safety is a priority when investigating anything that uses electricity, including ensuring they are unplugged and keeping these items away from water or wet hands.

Figure 6.15 A photo of an old phone, cardboard boxes and tubes, pens and Sellotape.
Source: Photograph taken by the author

Step by step:

■ Find a suitable place to explore the 'technological' object, such as at a table, on the floor or outside. Remember to stay safe, so disconnect the device during the exploration

■ Talk about the object you have chosen to explore. Do they know what it is and what it's used for? If you are exploring a vacuum cleaner, for example, try removing and replacing some of the parts, such as the handle, release it from the upright position and remove and replace the brush attachment – all of these things should make their own sounds. Invite your child to explore how many different sounds they can find. With other electronic devices, switching them on and off should elicit sounds from them, but this must always be properly supervised by an adult

- See if you and your child/children can mimic the sounds that you hear using your voices

Additional ideas:

- Gather some 'junk' e.g. cardboard boxes, foil, tubes, plastic containers and string to make your own pretend technological toy and mimic the noises you discovered when you played with your model.

Why?

This will focus your child's hearing and listening skills onto the sounds they are probably very accustomed to 'hearing' but very seldom notice. Tuning into sound is a vital prerequisite to learning about phonics sounds and subsequently using them to read and write.

Making other connections

The children will be very well supported with their understanding of technology with this activity and may well feel some confidence as children of this century! Therefore, skills in **Understanding the World** will be honed. It may also help some children to become familiar with some objects from their daily lives that they otherwise rarely pay attention to.

Listening Walk

Capture sounds from a walk to focus on later, perhaps at bedtime or on a long journey.

What you'll need:

■ A phone or device on which to record sounds that you hear when outside

■ Large jar or pot and 'counters' such as beads, coins, conkers or buttons (although always remember the safety of your children when using small items)

Figure 6.16 A photo of an adult and child listening to swans on a canal.
Source: Photograph taken by the author

Step by step:

■ Either whilst you and your child or children are out for a walk or whilst you are out walking alone, record some of the sounds you and your child are familiar with e.g. cars, buses, trains, aeroplanes, footsteps, dogs barking, doors closing, gates opening, birds, leaves in the trees, splashing in puddles . . . or sounds from inside your home e.g. washing machine, vacuum cleaner, taps running, doors opening or closing, toilet flushing . . .

■ This recording can be saved for a later time or used on the same day

■ Say to your child or children that you always hear so many sounds when you're out-side or in your home, and ask if they have ever noticed any

- Explain that you have some of these sounds on your phone/device and that you are going to challenge them to identify as many as they can! Whenever they get one right, they can put a 'counter' into the large pot

- Play the recorded sounds one at a time and see how many the children correctly identify

- At the end of the game, count up how many 'counters' the children collected in the pot

Additional ideas:

- You could encourage the children to describe the sounds they hear to support the expansion of their vocabulary e.g. scratchy, loud, soft, screeching . . .

Why?

This game will help the children to focus in on those daily sounds that can become 'invisible' as they become the background to our lives. Here, you will be helping the children to tune into those sounds, bringing them to the forefront of their minds.

Making other connections

There will be a strong connection here with **Understanding the World** as the children make connections in their experience and to the sounds they hear daily. **Literacy** skills will be supported with focused listening and making associations with familiar sounds, matching them with their existing knowledge.

7 Sounds We Make

In this chapter

In this chapter, the activities provide opportunities for children to make their own sounds. They will be encouraged to explore the quality (timbre) and dynamics of the sounds that they are creating or have created for them to listen to by their supporting adult.

Sounds We Make activities

DOI: 10.4324/9781003451082-10

Metal Sounds

This activity will help children focus very particularly on one type of sound.

What you'll need:

■ An array of metal objects to make sounds with e.g. pots, pans, bowls, spoons, buckets, plant pots and garden tools (ensuring they are all safe for children to handle)

Figure 7.1 A photograph of a collection of metal spoons, keys, kitchen utensils, tin, key and a wicker basket.
Source: Photograph taken by the author

Step by step:

■ Place all of your gathered metal objects in a basket, box or bag and have it beside you

■ Sit on the floor or at a table with your partner or group of children

10 min

- Gradually take your metal objects out of the bag or basket and place them in the space in front of you and the children. Engage the children in a discussion as you do so e.g. do they know what these things are? Have they seen any of them before? Can they imagine what they might be used for?

- Advise the children of any objects they need to be careful with

- Pick up an object and flick it with your finger. Ask the children if they can hear a sound. Talk about the sound you have made. Repeat with another object

- Invite the child or children to try flicking the objects for themselves. As they explore the metal objects, talk about any different sounds they can make and how they are making them

Additional ideas:

- To extend the activity, introduce 'beaters' to gently tap the metal items. The 'beaters' could be chopsticks, pencils, wooden spoons or straws, for example

Why?

This is a wonderful activity to help children realise that different things make different sounds, even when they have some common properties. Talk about the pitch of the sounds, are some high and tinkly? Do others making a deeper sound?

Making other connections

You will clearly be making connections within **Personal, Social and Emotional Development** through this social activity, but also good links with **Understanding the World** by helping the children to understand some of the properties of metal. You may well have a discussion about how the metal objects feel as you explore – they might realise that they are all cold and hard but can become warm as they are held!

Body Sound Rhymes

This is a fun, turn-taking game with a focus on sounds we can make ourselves.

What you'll need:

■ Make two spinners (see photo). On one, have pictures of body parts, and on the other, have images depicting nursery rhymes. Alternatively, you could use two dice with body parts/images for nursery rhymes or cards in two hats depicting body parts/images for rhymes

Figure 7.2 A photograph of two hats, a nursery rhyme dice and a body part spinner

Step by step:

■ Find a comfortable space to play the game with your child/children. This could be on the floor or at a table. You will need somewhere to roll the spinners or dice or to place the hats

- Explain that you will take turns to spin both spinners (roll both dice or take a card from each hat!)

- The person whose turn it is will take their turn to spin the spinners, then they will sing the nursery rhyme and use the body part they have selected to accompany the song e.g. sing 'Hickory Dickory Dock, the mouse ran up the clock . . .' whilst clapping their hands

- The person whose turn it is can choose whether to sing alone or if they would like you/others to join in

Additional ideas:

- To make this more challenging, you could make a list of how the body part is 'played' each time and make sure that each person makes a new/different sound if they select that same body part

Why?

It is good to internalise the rhythm, beat or pulse of the rhyme as it is sung or said. This will often emphasise the syllables, individual sounds and phrases that are being spoken, which will help children understand spoken language. This will support them when they come to read and write independently.

Making other connections

The links to **Literacy** are important, as explained in the 'why?' section, but also for **Expressive Arts and Design,** for children to develop a sense of rhythm musically. **Literacy** will again be supported with the breadth of vocabulary the children are exposed to through the rhymes, and **Personal, Social and Emotional Development** will be explored through the turn-taking aspect of the activity.

Body Sound Stories

Another opportunity to have fun joining together by creating a soundtrack to your favourite stories!

What you'll need:

■ Your voices and bodies for this activity!

Figure 7.3 A photograph of three wooden spoons painted as pigs on a wicker basket.
Source: Photograph taken by the author

Step by step:

■ Sit with your child or children. This game can be played anywhere you have a moment to fill – indoors, outside or on the move!

■ Choose a story to tell. Fairy tales are great stories to use with this activity, especially those with a repetitive nature, such as 'The Three Little Pigs'

- Explain to the children that you will need their help to tell the story by making sounds for the characters and events

- Model how to add sounds to the stories to the children first, and if they are able, they could help you to invent the sounds you need e.g. the wolf (a growl), the first little pig (a high-pitched 'oink'), the third little pig (a low-pitched 'oink'), the straw (rub your hands together) and the bricks (pat your knees)

- Tell the story to the children and encourage them to help you add in the sounds as they occur

Additional ideas:

- If you have a piece of large paper and some pens, you could make a 'key' of the sounds for each event or character in your story to help you all remember. These could be made into a Sound Story Book!

- As the children grow in confidence, you could scribe the story and they could draw in the actions

Why?

Listening to a story without using pictures or books to support the telling is a great skill for children to learn. It will help to develop their listening skills and also encourage them to use their imaginations – visualising the pictures in their minds!

Making other connections

There are strong connections with **Literacy** development in the children being able to listen to a story, visualise events and eventually retell the story for themselves. Also, with the story being scribed, modelling writing and the children making their own marks, too. **Expressive Arts and Design** development with the musical skill of adding a soundtrack to the story. An **IT** element could easily be added if you record or video the story to listen to or share with others later.

Voice Tappers

This activity is an extension to Dapper Tappers and Tap Tap Tappers but uses some vocal skills, too.

What you'll need:

- Six (or 12) 'beaters' that are safe for children to play with, such as wooden and metal spoons, jug mops, washing up brushes, scrubbing brushes, paint brushes of differing sizes, chopsticks (supervised according to age), pencils, makeup or pastry brushes, sticks, plastic and/or metal whisk . . .

- A bag or box to hold the 'beaters'

- A dice (or two) with different pictures of the 'beaters' on each side

- A box or any large item suitable to be the 'drum' to be tapped

Figure 7.4 A photograph of a child making a voice sound.
Source: Photograph taken by the author

Step by step:

- Sit with your child or with a group of children in a circle

- Show the children the dice and the pictures of 'beaters' that are drawn on them

- Show them the selection of matching 'beaters' and place them, the dice and the 'drum' in the centre of the circle

- Choose a child to start the game by rolling a die. That child then selects the matching 'beater' from the selection you have shared and taps the 'drum' in the middle of the circle

- Invite the children to make a sound that matches the tapped sound with their voices e.g. 'duff, duff, duff' or 'twack, twack'. Encourage the children to be as inventive as they like!

- Talk about which sound is the hardest to make

Additional ideas:

- Two children could roll dice during the same 'turn'. Place an additional 'drum' in the middle of the circle, then tap both together. The children then choose which sound to make! A voice-tapping orchestra and choir!

Why?

This activity will encourage the children to really listen to the quality of the sound, its timbre and its volume. This will stretch and hone their listening skills further. Adding their own voice to the activity ensures they are all engaged in what is happening and need to focus to take part.

Making other connections

Elements of **Personal, Social and Emotional Development** will be explored with the social nature of the game and the 'rules' are adhered to, encouraging self-awareness and regulation. **Expressive Arts and Design** is developed through focused attention to the sounds. With children who are ready, the words 'timbre' and 'dynamics' could be introduced to build their vocabulary.

Hidden Instrument Sounds

It will be best if the children are familiar with the instrument that you use for this game. The children will love guessing the sounds!

What you'll need:

- A selection of simple musical instruments
- A screen (two chairs and a duvet cover) or a large cardboard box

Figure 7.5 A photograph of simple percussion instruments inside a wicker basket.
Source: Photograph taken by the author

Step by step:

- Sit somewhere spacious where you can arrange the instruments behind your 'screen', and your child or children can sit and not see your instruments!

Sounds We Make

- Explain that you are going to play a guessing game. You are secretly going to play an instrument, and the children are going to guess which instrument it is that you are playing

- Remind the children to sit quietly and really listen! If you are working with a group of children, let them know who you are going to ask first. They will take turns

- Play your first instrument and see if the children can guess which it is

- If they are right, show them the instrument and play the game again, choosing a different instrument. If they are not right, talk about the sound the instrument makes before carrying on with the game

- Keep playing until all of the instruments have been guessed, then allow the children some time to explore freely with the instruments

Additional ideas:

- The correct 'guesser' could be the next person to play the instrument for everyone else to guess

---

Why?

This game will really focus the children on the sounds that the individual instruments make, defining and honing their auditory skills.

Making other connections

Personal, Social and Emotional Development skills will be honed with the turn-taking aspect of this game, bolstering that executive function. Both **Expressive Arts and Design and Understanding the World** will be supported with the naming of the instruments, building vocabulary and knowledge.

Circle Sounds

What you'll need:

- Just you and a child or small group of children

- As e.g. mouth, nose, hands, feet, elbow, fingers (anything that can be used to make a sound)

- A small, smooth pebble

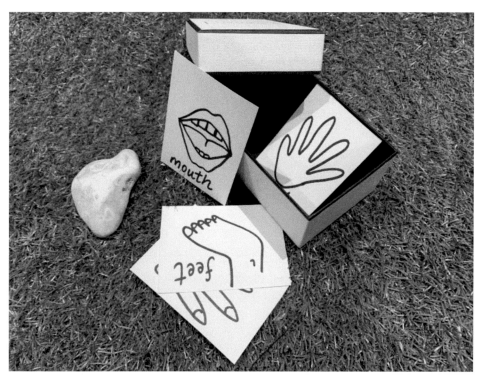

Figure 7.6 A photograph of a pebble, a box and some body part cards on grass.
Source: Photograph taken by the author

Step by step:

- Chant this rhyme:

    - *'Pass the pebble round and round,*

    - *Careful not to make a sound,*

    - *Pass it on and when it stops,*

    - *Then we look inside the box!'*

- Show the children a smooth, small pebble that you will pass around the circle/or back and forth as you say the rhyme. Whoever is holding the pebble as you finish the rhyme will put the pebble down and choose a card from the box

- That child then has to make a loud sound with whichever body part is drawn on the card they choose

- When they have made the sound, everyone else copies the sound they made; the card is then replaced in the box, and the game continues. Start the rhyme again and continue passing the pebble around the circle/or back and forth

- Continue the game until everyone has had a turn or several turns

Additional ideas:

- If you'd like to sing, the chant could be sung to the tune of 'Boys and Girls come out to play', 'Humpty Dumpty sat on a wall' or even 'Bobby Shaftoe'

- If your child or children are able, they could be encouraged to make a rhythmic sound to the noises they are making, then everyone could join in with the repeating pattern e.g. tap tap tap . . . tap tap tap . . . with their feet or 'oo oo oooo, oo oo oooo' with their mouth/voice sound

Why?

Here, you will be teaching the children a new chant or song. The game encourages the children to be inventive with voice sounds, create new sounds, listen carefully to others to recreate their sounds and tune into sound in an engaging activity.

Making other connections

Literacy learning is enhanced by the learning of the new rhyme and **Expressive Arts and Design** if you add a tune. **Mathematical** development will be supported if you choose to add the repeated pattern element to the sounds that are made.

Dice Beaters

Children will love playing the instruments but with a focus this time on what they are being played with!

What you'll need:

■ A range of 'beaters' to play the instruments with e.g. commercially made beaters, washing up brushes of various types, paint brushes of varying size, chopsticks, wooden spoons, straws, feathers, dried grasses, dried bullrushes . . .

■ A homemade die – use a plain wooden cube or make your own die from card

■ Draw or stick pictures of the different beaters on the dice

■ A range of musical instruments in a basket or box

Figure 7.7 A photograph of some simple percussion instruments, a bucket containing a whisk, a wooden spoon, two brushes, chopsticks, a spoon and a die.
Source: Photograph taken by the author

Step by step:

■ Sit on the floor or in a comfortable place with your partner or group of children. Make sure there is space to roll the die

■ Before you start the game, take the instruments out of the box or basket and share them with the children, saying the name of each e.g. castanets, tambour . . .

- Show the children the beaters. Spend time explaining that you will be using the beaters to play the instruments, but take this opportunity to emphasise that the children must be gentle and respectful when playing the instruments

- Explain that you will take turns to roll the die. Whichever picture is on the top when the die has been rolled is the beater they will use. They can choose any instrument that they would like to play. Only that person takes their turn playing, and it is the next person's turn to roll the die

- When it is their turn, the children can find any way they like to play and explore the instrument using the beater. Can they find a new and interesting way to play?

- As the instruments are explored, talk about the sounds they make and how they differ from each other. Try to find or invent words to describe the sounds

Additional ideas:

- You could start this activity with just one or two instruments so as not to overwhelm the children with too many choices. Build up the supply of instruments as they become more experienced

- You could make two dice and have the instruments on the other dice. The children then roll two dice to make their choices

Why?

Using the beaters will enable the children to make a whole new array of sounds with the same collection of instruments. Always make sure to talk about the sounds being made with the children.

Making other connections

As well as **Personal, Social and Emotional Development** and **Communication and Language**, you will be adding elements of **Expressive Arts and Design** as the children explore methods of playing the instruments. Always encourage the children to learn the correct names of the instruments, e.g. 'maracas' rather than 'a rattle' or 'shaker', to broaden their vocabulary and general knowledge.

Dice Instruments

Children always love to play musical instruments. This activity enables them to try a variety of instruments.

What you'll need:

■ A homemade die – use a plain wooden cube or make your own die or spinner from card

■ Draw or stick pictures of musical instruments on the die or spinner

■ A basket or box containing the same instruments as are on the die

Figure 7.8 A photograph of wooden musical instruments in a wicker basket with a die.
Source: Photograph taken by the author

Step by step:

■ Sit on the floor or in a comfortable place with your partner or group of children. Make sure there is space to roll the die or to spin the spinner

15 min

- Before you start the game, take the instruments out of the box or basket and share them with the children, saying the name of each e.g. castanets, tambour. Resist the temptation to play the instruments at this time!

- Explain that you will take turns to roll the die. Whichever picture is on the top when the die has been rolled is the picture of the instrument that person needs to play. Only that person takes their turn playing, and then it is the next person's turn to roll the die

- When it is their turn, the children can find any way they like to play and explore the instrument; the greater variety of sounds they can find, the better!

- As the instruments are explored, talk about the sounds they make and how they differ from each other. Try to find or invent words to describe the sounds

Additional ideas:

- To provide an 'end' to each person's turn, another person in the group could be the 'conductor'. They are given a sound maker that is different from those in the box or basket, such as some jingle bells. When the person whose turn it is has explored and played their instrument for a few moments, they ring the bells and it will be time for the next person to roll the die

- You could make two dice so the person who rolls them chooses a friend to play the instruments together. Talk about the similarities and differences between the sounds

Why?

This is a fun and sociable way to encourage children to explore musical instruments. You will be able to draw their attention to the sounds they make and celebrate the new sounds they find!

Making other connections

This will support **Personal, Social and Emotional Development**, encouraging children to take turns and take account of others. They will learn to self-regulate as they wait for their turn – instruments are very exciting, so it will take a lot of self-control to wait!

Fabric Fun!

This activity will not only encourage listening, but also some large and small movements, so it adds a physical development aspect.

What you'll need:

- A selection of fabrics: for example, cotton, lace, chiffon, hessian, canvas, florist's ribbon, silver heat blanket, satin, manmade fabrics, velvet, muslin, taffeta, corduroy, organza, voile . . .

Figure 7.9 A photograph of a collection of fabrics – foil, blue cotton, hessian, stripey towel, chiffon and a net curtain.
Source: Photograph taken by the author

Step by step:

- Sit on the floor or at a table with your partner or group of children

- Introduce the fabrics to your child or children, touching them and talking about how they feel. If they are older, share the fabric names with them

- Encourage the child or children to talk about how the different fabrics feel when they touch them

- Now, start to listen to the sounds the fabrics make when they are moved. Encourage the children to move the fabric in different ways to change the sounds – move them slowly and gently or rub them against the same fabric and different fabrics to see if the sounds change. Wave them in the air – sometimes slowly and smoothly or try 'snapping' them quickly to make a louder sound

- Introduce some descriptive language such as rustling, squeaking, crinkling, snapping, whooshing, long or short, crackling, fizzing, popping . . .

Additional ideas:

- Make a recording of the different sounds, then play it back to the children to see if they can match the sound to the fabric

- Try ripping some of the fabric. Not all fabric will tear easily, so making a starting snip with scissors might help. The sound can be very satisfying!

Why?

It's good to use resources that wouldn't normally be associated with sound. This will encourage children to tune into other sounds around them that they would normally ignore in their day-to-day lives.

Making other connections

This activity will help **Physical Development** as the children learn to manipulate the fabrics. Smaller movements will help small muscle development (fine motor skills), and larger movements will help larger muscles in arms and shoulders (gross motor skills). Tearing fabric will help both hand and arm muscles, depending on the fabric.

High Chair Sounds

Your child can enjoy this activity whilst spending time with you in the kitchen.

What you'll need:

■ A high chair with a tray or chair attached to a table so there is a flat surface in front of the child

Figure 7.10 A photograph of a child's hands on a table.
Source: Photograph taken by the author

Step by step:

- Place your child in the high chair and ensure they are safe and securely strapped in

- Model how to make sounds on the flat surface in front of your child

- Tap or scrape with your fingertips, your knuckles and your palm, each time expressing joy at the sound you have made

- Name the sounds as you make them e.g. 'ooooo, tick, tick, tick' or 'oh wow, splat splat splat' to make it fun!

- Encourage your child to do the same and express joy at their sounds

Additional ideas:

- Do this activity regularly, encouraging your child to make the voice sounds to go with the hand sounds they are making

- Try doing this in different places, such as on the grass if sitting outside, in the bath or when on a train or bus journey

Why?

This will encourage your child to realise that they can have an effect on their surroundings and can make many different sounds. With your help, they will learn that different sounds can be heard in different places. This will support them in making that all-important auditory discrimination.

Making other connections

This activity will help in **Physical Development,** moving, handling and using their hands independently for a purpose, gaining control over their movements. **Communication and Language** will be supported through the making of sounds to accompany their percussive sound-making and using new words to describe the sounds made!

How Loud Is that Sound?

This activity will help children to focus very particularly on the quality and dynamics of a sound. **This is best played after the children have experienced both the Metal Sounds and Wooden Sounds activities.**

What you'll need:

■ Gather together a selection of the metal and wooden objects you have previously used to make sounds (and add some plastic ones!) e.g. pots, pans, plastic or metal bowls, spoons, buckets, plastic containers, logs, flower pots (ensuring they are all safe and unbreakable! This activity might mean items are tapped quite hard!)

■ A bag to hold the objects you have gathered

Figure 7.11 A photograph of a child with their hands on their ears laughing.
Source: Photograph taken by the author

Step by step:

■ Place all of your gathered wooden, metal and plastic objects in a basket, box or bag and place it beside you

Sounds We Make

- Sit on the floor or at a table with your partner or group of children

- Gradually take the objects out of the bag and place them in the space in front of you and the children. Engage the children in a discussion as you do so e.g. do they remember the objects? Can they remember what they are normally used for? What are they called?

- Remind the children of any objects they need to be careful with

- Tap an object to make a sound. Ponder aloud, 'I wonder if I can make this sound louder?' See if the children have any ideas as to how this could happen or simply model making it louder for younger children. What do you need to do to make the sound as loud as you can? **Remind the children about safety and ensure all are safe at all times throughout this activity.**

- See how the loudest sound can be made and who can make it!

Additional ideas:

- If you have undertaken this activity inside, try taking it outside, where the acoustics will be completely different. Talk about how the sound has changed outdoors

Why?

This is a great activity for children to have the freedom to be noisy and explore how to make really loud sounds! It helps the children get to grips with 'cause and effect'. It's important they are able to make as much noise as possible on occasion – so often we ask them to be quiet!

Making other connections

This activity will be connected with **Understanding the World** as children freely explore sound and dynamics, which materials are making the loudest sounds and how we can make that happen.

Spin-a-Sound

This activity will engage children in using the body sounds they are starting to discover in a fun way.

What you'll need:

■ A spinner (homemade from a hexagon/octagon of card with a pencil in the middle – with a body part pictured on each side – see Figure 7.12)

Figure 7.12 A photograph of a spinner with body parts on it.
Source: Photograph taken by the author

Step by step:

■ Sit on the floor or at a table with your partner or group of children

■ Before you start the game, make sure everyone knows how to spin the spinner. Have a practice

131

- Explain how the game will work. Each of you takes a turn to spin the spinner, and the turn-taker must make a sound with whichever body part the spinner lands on!

- All of the other players then make the same sound

- The person to the left of the spinner then takes their turn

- Encourage everyone to make a new sound with the body part that the spinner lands on

Additional ideas:

- To give the game an ending, you could have a pile of counters, beads or beans in the centre. Each time someone has a turn, they take a bead and you continue until all of the beads have been used

- Each person then counts their beans to see if they have the same amount (adding a great maths element to the game!). If the numbers are different, the challenge could be how to make them the same the next time

Why?

It's important that children understand that their bodies can make sounds and hear the difference between these sounds. Talk to them about this as you play the game. The sounds they generate now will come in useful later on in making rhythms.

Making other connections

This activity will help develop skills in **Personal, Social and Emotional Development.** Children will learn to take turns with others and to wait patiently – supporting self-regulation. They will enjoy the social fun of joining in the sound-making with others. Skills in **Communication and Language** will develop through conversation as they play and use new words to describe the sounds made!

Unwrap the Sounds

Always remember to keep children safe when they are engaging with small objects. Supervise them carefully throughout the activity.

What you'll need:

■ A selection of small objects that will make a sound (or not!) e.g. keys, pieces of dried pasta, pens, teaspoons, coins, buttons, feathers, cotton wool balls or screws. Keep one of each item on one side for use in the game

■ A number of small boxes to place the items in

■ Paper to wrap up the boxes e.g. Christmas or birthday paper or simple brown paper and string or tape

Figure 7.13 A photograph of two wrapped boxes, rings, coins, feathers, tape, string, ribbon and scissors.
Source: Photograph taken by the author

15 min

Step by step:

- Place each different sort of sound maker into a different box, i.e. the pasta in one box, the keys in another

- Wrap up each box with paper

- Gather your children together and tell them that you have placed some things in the boxes and wrapped them up, but you have forgotten what you placed in each box! You will need their help to find them, and you think that the best way to do it is by listening carefully to the sounds the boxes make

- Tell them that the first thing you need to find is your keys. Can they find the box that contains your keys?

- When they have been discovered, place a key on top of the box so you don't forget what you decided. Then, say what you are looking for next, perhaps the buttons

- Once all the boxes have been decided, invite the children to open them carefully to see if they were right!

Additional ideas:

- The children could make their own secret boxes, wrapping them up for their friends to play the game

Why?

This game will excite the children and encourage them to listen really carefully to the sounds in the boxes. The added excitement of unwrapping a 'present' always adds to the fun.

Making other connections

The main activity will hone the children's listening skills, so it will add to their **Literacy Development**. If they choose to engage in the 'additional idea', they will also be honing their fine motor skills, which will add to their **Physical Development.**

Animal Orchestra

This could be shared as an adult-guided activity, then it could be honed and explored further during their independent play.

What you'll need:

- Small world animals and additional props e.g. 'grass', fabric, logs, etc.

- Some cards to make a 'trumpet' to amplify your voice sounds

- A chopstick

Figure 7.14 A photograph of a card trumpet, small world animals, grass, wooden houses, a wicker basket and some hessian.
Source: Photograph taken by the author

Step by step:

- Invite your child or children to sit with you in a comfortable space with the animals and additional props in front of you on the floor or table

- Play with the animals together for a little while, chatting as you do so, then ask the children if they know the sounds that some of the animals make

- Take time to make some of the sounds and listen as the children make them, too. Then, suggest that you make cones from the card to make trumpets to make the sounds louder

- When they have made their trumpets, see if they can make each animal sound as you point to the animals e.g. 'mooooooo' or 'baaaaaaa' or 'oink oink'

- You could become an animal orchestra as the children only make the sound when you, as the 'conductor', point to the animals. You could do this with your 'baton' (chopstick!). Suggest that they only make the sound whilst you are actually pointing to the animal

- Allow the children to take the role of the 'conductor' of the animal orchestra

Additional ideas:

- The children could decorate their homemade trumpets or make others that are more fantastic and see the sounds that they make

- You could assign an animal to a child, and they play a 'solo' when their animal is pointed to

- Draw a large 'stave' (five parallel lines on which music is written) and place the animals on the stave as though they are real music!

Why?

This game will excite the children and encourage them to recreate sounds they are familiar with, changing the sounds with the use of their 'trumpets'.

Making other connections

This activity will hone skills in **Literacy** as the children recreate and listen to the sounds being made to represent the animals. **Expressive Arts and Design** will be a real focus with the music-making and creating their own homemade trumpets.

Sock Shakers

It's always fun to play with socks. The brighter the socks, the better!

What you'll need:

■ Gather together some old socks (make sure they don't have holes!) and fill them with things that will make a sound, such as rice, pasta, lentils, wooden beads, foil, pebbles, seeds, conkers, acorns, etc. and tie them securely at the top – you could use rubber bands, or hairbands for this

■ Create a number of socks that you will use that have the same contents as those you are sharing with the children. Place these in a separate box

If you are using small items with small children, ensure the socks are tied securely to prevent the risk of a child choking should the items come out of the socks

Figure 7.15 A photograph of some socks, hairbands, buttons, bamboo tubes, pasta, coins and bottle tops.
Source: Photograph taken by the author

Step by step:

■ Sit in a comfortable space with your child or children and place the socks in front of you on the floor or table. Encourage your child or children to explore the socks. They will discover that they have things inside, so encourage them to shake them to make sounds

■ After they have explored the socks for a while, suggest that they choose their favourite one or two to 'play' whilst you sing. You could sing songs or nursery rhymes whilst you accompany yourselves with the sock orchestra

■ Encourage the children to place their socks back on the floor or table and select a sock from your box. Shake your sock and ask if the children can find one of their socks that makes a matching sound. Repeat this activity with all of your socks until they are all matched

Additional ideas:

■ Leave the sock orchestra in your learning space for the children to play with independently and invent their own games

■ As you play with the socks, see if the children can copy your beat or rhythm with their own socks

Why?

This activity uses very familiar items in different ways, which will be fun for the children. They will use all of their auditory skills to listen carefully to the sounds they are hearing and to match them.

Making other connections

Personal, Social and Emotional Development will be supported as the children work together to play music with others and to match the sounds. Their autonomy will be bolstered as they work independently with the socks following the activity, possibly sharing their knowledge with others, too!

Rat-a-Tap-Tap

This activity will require some work beforehand to make some homemade drums.

What you'll need:

■ A selection of drums that the children have made prior to this activity. These could be very simple, such as upturned cake tins or storage boxes, or more elaborate ones that the children have made and decorated from junk materials, such as empty ice cream or butter containers, cereal boxes or empty crisp/snack containers

Figure 7.16 A photograph of a cake tin, two plastic boxes, a wooden box and a fabric box on a wooden table.
Source: Photograph taken by the author

Step by step:

■ Sit somewhere spacious where you will all have room to play your 'drums'

■ Before you start playing the game, allow your child or children to explore their drum, sharing with each other how they made it and the sound/s it makes

- Explain that you are going to sing some songs and play your drums as you do so. You may need to teach the simple songs if the children are not familiar with them. Songs such as 'This is the way we play our drum, play our drum, play our drum . . . on a cold and frosty morning' or 'This old man, he played one, he played nick knack on his drum, with a nick knack paddy whack give the dog a bone, this old man came rolling home'. There are other songs you could sing and drum to, such as 'Peter hammers with one hammer . . .' or 'It's raining it's pouring . . .' or 'I hear thunder, I hear thunder, hark don't you . . . ?' which are also great drumming songs!

- Sing the songs together and play your drums

Additional ideas:

- You could introduce some of the 'beaters' you might have used in other activities, such as feathers, paint brushes or wooden spoons

- Don't forget to have your own homemade drum, too!

- You could record your music and see if the children can hear their own drums as you play it back to them!

Why?

This is a fabulous activity to support not only the children's auditory discrimination by listening to the sounds they make but also having made their drums, which they are then using for a very real purpose.

Making other connections

Personal, Social and Emotional Development skills will be honed as the children play together in their own homemade drum orchestra as well as the musical and performance elements of **Expressive Arts and Design.**

Roll-a-Sound

This can be a speedy game full of lots of body sound action!

What you'll need:

- A die, either spotty or numbered (you could make spinners or simply write numbers on small squares of paper and place them in a container to be selected when it's somebody's turn)

- A large piece of white card and a marker pen to draw body parts on and write numbers beside them

Figure 7.17 A photograph of a piece of paper with numbered body parts drawn on it.
Source: Photograph taken by the author

Step by step:

- Find a comfortable space to play the game with your child/children. This could be on the floor or at a table. You will need somewhere to roll die

- You could prepare the sheet of body parts and numbers before you start, or you might like to do this with the children

- Explain that the first child will roll the die and then find out from the chart, by matching their number, which body part they will need to make a sound with! You could demonstrate how the game will work

- The first child takes their turn and makes a body sound. After they have made the sound, the rest of the group could echoes the sound back to them. The next child then takes their turn, and the game continues

- Encourage the children to invent new sounds with each turn!

Additional ideas

- You could use two dice or spinners, and then the children would need to use two body parts at the same time e.g. hands and feet!

Why?

This game will ensure the children are active and moving whilst they are learning. They focus on a body part and use it to make a sound, think about that sound and work out how to create it. They listen to the sound that is made, tuning into it.

Making other connections

The links to **Physical Development** come with movement and activity. This is a social activity, too, so elements of **Personal, Social and Emotional Development** will be honed.

Dice Numbered Instruments

An exciting game for two or more players, where a range of musical instruments will be played.

What you'll need:

- A selection of up to six simple musical instruments
- Some numbered cards (either spotty or with numerals)
- A die (either spotty or with numerals)

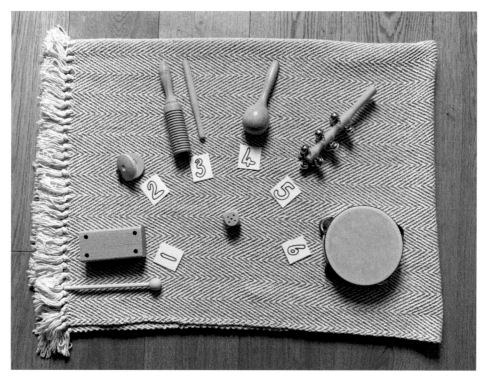

Figure 7.18 A photograph of a blanket with musical instruments with numbers from 1 to 6.
Source: Photograph taken by the author

Step by step:

- Find a comfortable space to play the game with your child or children (and a space where others won't be disturbed!)
- Place the instruments in a line on the floor or table and place a number card in front of each instrument

Sounds We Make

- Go through the instruments with the child/children, making sure they know the name of each one. Go through the number cards

- Show the children the die and explain that they will roll the die and whichever number is facing upwards, they need to play the instrument with the matching number

- Take turns to roll the die and play the instruments

- To provide some challenge, another child (or the adult) could suggest a way to play the instrument e.g. slowly, sparkly, gently, madly!

Additional ideas:

- If you create two dice, then more instruments could be added to the game as the numbers are added together

- You could have the 'stop playing' indicator, such as a loud drum or bells (a different instrument from those being played in the game). When this is played, the child stops playing their instrument and it will be the next person's turn. Eventually, another child could assume this role

Why?

This is a lovely way to ensure children experience playing a lot of different instruments and are exposed to the different sounds they make. Choosing ways for them to play the instruments will enable children to hear and respond to a broad and rich vocabulary.

Making other connections

Expressive Arts and Design will be supported by the range of instruments being played in the different ways suggested – altering their speed and dynamics.
Mathematics Development will be contextualised with the recognition of numbers and/or subitising (knowing a number from the pattern of the dots on the die).

Picture Book Alliteration

This activity will enhance the sharing of books with no words and support the recognition of initial sounds. It will be best if you can familiarise yourself with the picture book or picture/photograph before undertaking this activity.

What you'll need:

■ Choose a book, or books, without pictures. If you don't have any, you could always use a book with words and 'busy' illustrations or an interesting picture or photograph to play this game

Figure 7.19 A photograph of some books on a blanket with letter cards, s m b c on top.
Source: Photograph taken by the author

Step by step:

■ Sit somewhere that is comfortable and cosy with your child or group of children

■ Invite them to choose a book if you have a selection of them to hand, or share the book or picture you have ready. Introduce the book or picture by talking about the front cover, what you see, what you think it might be about

- Tell the children that you have a great game that you can play – suggest that it's a spying game or a sound hunt (something that sounds exciting!)

- Say that the first sound you are going to hunt for is a 'b', for example. They have got to find as many things as they can that begin with that sound

- You could model the writing of the words they come up with, and if they are beginning to understand graphemes, draw their attention to the shape of the initial letter of each word and talk about them all being the same

- If your children are ready for oral blending, then you could sound out the rest of the word, annunciating the first sound so it is louder than the rest e.g. '**B**-u-g' or '**B**-r-ea-d'

Additional ideas:

- You could have a sand timer (or other timer) to make the hunt more exciting – they need to find as many objects as they can before the time is up!

- You could play the 'I Spy' rhyme game in this way – find an object in the picture and say, 'I spy with my little eye, something that rhymes with . . .'

Why?

Here, you are focusing the children's attention specifically on the initial sounds in the words. This is an important part of early reading, hearing and saying the first letter in a word. This is an important strategy when they are orally and visually blending independently.

Making other connections

The connections here are with **Understanding the World** as you talk about, investigate and scrutinise the pictures, discussing what you see, why something might be there and providing new vocabulary that the children might not all yet know. If you use a timer, then a clear link is made with **Mathematical Development.**

Instrument Board Game

This activity will engage the children in a turn-taking dice game. Teach the children the 'proper' names for the instruments and let them know that they need to treat the instruments with respect; otherwise, they will break.

What you'll need:

- A simple homemade board for the game (see Figure 7.20). Your board can have as many squares as is appropriate for the age and concentration of your child/children. Draw or place pictures of musical instruments in each square. Number each square. Note where the game starts and finishes

- A die with numbers 1, 2 and 3 on it

- A 'counter' for each player – borrowed from another game, or you could use shells, buttons or small pebbles

- The musical instruments that you have on the board

Figure 7.20 A photograph of some wooden instruments, a board for the game with instruments and numbers in squares and a blue drawstring bag.
Source: Photograph taken by the author

Step by step:

- Explain to your child or children that you are going to play a board game. You will take it in turns to roll the die and then move your 'counter' over your board for as many squares as the number that is facing upwards on your die

- The first player rolls the dice, then moves their counter that many squares, and whatever picture they land on, that is the musical instrument they must play/make a sound with

- It is then the next person's turn. The game continues until somebody reaches the finish!

Additional ideas:

- The person whose turn it is could choose a friend to play an instrument with at the same time. This could be an identical instrument or a different one. If it is an identical one, then you need to make sure you provide two of each instrument at the beginning!

- The player whose turn it is makes a sound, perhaps a rhythm pattern the other person copies back to them e.g. tap-tap-tap, tap-tap-tap . . . which their friend echoes back to them

- Make a bigger board, then you could use a die with numbers up to six

- Use a spotty die so the children can practice subitising (knowing the number instantly from the pattern of the dots without counting)

Why?

This game will give children time to use the musical instruments and explore the sounds they can make with them. They will experience some agency (control) if they are playing a sound that their companion then has to imitate.

Making other connections

There are clear connections with **Mathematics** in this game with the subitising and 'counting on' from a number. **Personal, Social and Emotional Development** will be enhanced with the turn-taking aspect. **Expressive Arts and Design** will be enhanced by exploring and trying new ways to play the musical instruments.

Body Sound Board Game

This activity will engage the children in a turn-taking dice game.

What you'll need:

- A simple homemade board for the game (see Figure 7.21). Your board can have as many squares as is appropriate for the age and concentration of your child/children. Draw body parts in each square. Number each square. Note where the game starts and finishes

- A dice with numbers 1, 2 and 3 on it

- A 'counter' for each player – borrowed from another game, or you could use shells, buttons or small pebbles

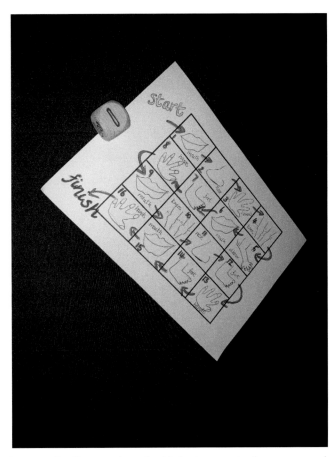

Figure 7.21 A photograph of a game board with body parts in the squares and a wooden dice.
Source: Photograph taken by the author

Step by step:

- Explain to your child or children that you are going to play a board game. You will take it in turns to roll the dice and then move your 'counter' over your board for as many squares as the number that is facing upwards on your die

- The first player rolls the die, then moves their counter that many squares, and whatever picture they land on, that is the body part they must make a sound with

- It is then the next person's turn. The game continues until somebody reaches the finish!

Additional ideas:

- The other players could mimic the sound made by the player whose turn it is

- The player who makes the sound could make a rhythm pattern that the other copies back to them e.g. clap, clap, clap-clap-clap

- Make a bigger board, then you could use a dice with numbers up to six

- Use a spotty dice so the children can practice subitising (knowing the number instantly from the pattern of the dots without counting!)

Why?

This game will reinforce other work the children have done on creating body sounds and encourage them to make new ones! Taking turns is an important skill, as is 'moving on' from your space when playing dice games.

Making other connections

There are very clear connections with **Mathematics** in this game with the subitising and 'counting on' from a number. **Personal, Social and Emotional Development** will be enhanced with the turn-taking aspect and for each child not always being the winner and to celebrate the success of others. Everyone will be actively involved as they and others make the body sounds.

Clickbox Sounds

This activity might keep a small child amused whilst sitting in a high chair.

What you'll need:

- A selection of plastic storage containers

- A selection of things to go inside the containers that will make a variety of sounds e.g. pasta, lentils, rice, leaves, small stones, teaspoons, feathers, shells, acorns, conkers, sticks and lolly sticks . . .

Figure 7.22 A photograph of some plastic containers with pasta, cornflakes and raisins inside on a wooden table.
Source: Photograph taken by the author

Step by step:

- Place the objects in the boxes and ensure they are securely closed. This activity should be supervised to ensure the safety of small children

■ Choose one of the boxes and place it in front of your children, shaking it as you do so

■ Encourage your child to shake the box too whilst you model comments about the sound such as 'Oo, what a loud sound that makes!', or 'Wow, that's a really scrapey sound' or whisper, 'Isn't that a really quiet sound?'

■ Place another box in front of your child and encourage them to explore the sound in that box. Encourage your children to compare the two sounds

■ You can add more boxes if your child is interested. Over time, you could explore more/different sound boxes. Always ensure you draw your child's attention to the sounds the boxes make

■ As they become more exposed to the sounds, see if they can match them e.g. share a box of feathers and see if they can find another really quiet sound. Or find two boxes that have really loud sounds in them

Additional ideas:

■ You could start to sing a song or nursery rhyme and encourage your child to play one of the boxes to accompany your singing. You could have one or two each. Create a Clickbox Orchestra!

Why?

This game will help your child to start tuning into sounds around them. They will start to realise that sounds can be heard anywhere, which will support them tuning into sounds at other times during their day. Sounds are all around us, and they will learn to discriminate between them with this focus on listening.

Making other connections

This activity will support **Physical Development** as children learn to manipulate and shake the boxes, especially if they accompany singing and start to shake in response to the rhythm of the song. This type of shaking will naturally, in most children, take the form of shaking to the pulse of the syllables, supporting further **Literacy** skill development.

8 Sounds With Words

In this chapter

In this chapter, the activities provide opportunities for children to use their voices to sing songs and nursery rhymes. There are some activities that include the use of books – some with text and others without.

Sounds with Words

DOI: 10.4324/9781003451082-11

Sounds With Words

Around a Rhyme

In this activity, the children will develop some physical skills alongside listening to and singing rhymes and songs.

What you'll need:

- A length of rope, ribbon, some lycra, an old scrunchy hose pipe – something long that children can hold in a circle. If there are a very small number of you, you could use a hula hoop

- A smaller piece of ribbon or a large peg (the sort used for den-making would be perfect – see Figure 8.1)

Figure 8.1 A photograph of a child and adult holding a hula hoop.
Source: Photograph taken by the author

Step by step:

- Gather your child or children around the circle of fabric, rope or your hoop and invite them to hold it with both hands

- Tie a ribbon or attach a peg to one place on the circle of fabric, rope or your hoop

■ Explain to the children that you are going to sing a song as you pass the 'circle' around, and when you finish the song, the person with the ribbon or peg in front of them is going to choose a rhyme or song for you all to sing together

■ The song you will sing as you pass the 'circle' around is:

'Pass the circle pass it on
When it stops we'll sing a song
Keep on passing round the ring
When it stops we will all sing
Pass the circle pass it on
Now it's stopped we'll sing a song'
(to the tune of Twinkle Twinkle Little Star)

■ Whoever has the ribbon or peg in front of them at the end of the song chooses a song to sing, and everyone will join in as it is sung

Additional ideas:

■ If your children are very young and/or you think they might struggle to think of a nursery rhyme or song for you all to sing, then place some props in the centre of the circle that might prompt them. You could use nursery rhyme wooden spoons or cards with pictures on them or items that remind them of songs, such as a toy black sheep, a spider (eensy weensy), etc.

Why?

This game will encourage the use and knowledge of a range of nursery rhymes, all picking out different rhyming words at the end of the lines of the song. Children will naturally tune into these rhymes, tuning into similar sounds that will support their later phonic learning.

Making other connections

This activity will help develop skills in **Physical Development** if you use something heavier, such as a rope, for the children to pass around. This will develop their hand/upper body/arm/shoulder strength – all good preparation for holding a pencil and writing!

Tell a Story, Make It Up!

This is quite a challenging activity, so perhaps it is good for children who are a little older or ready to hold things in their memory!

What you'll need:

- A selection of objects that all start with the same sound e.g. sausage, sweet, sun, sock, sunflower, skeleton . . .

- A soft toy (teddy) or something equally interesting to pass around the circle or between you

Figure 8.2 A photo of a child sitting on carpet playing with a small soft toy dog.
Source: Photograph taken by the author

Step by step:

- Invite your child or children to sit with you in a circle if you are in a group. Place your selection of objects in front of you all. Talk about the objects and 'discover' together that they all start with the same sound!

- Explain that you are all together going to tell a story that is about the sound 'sssssss' (if that is your sound), and it will include all of the objects that are in front of you. You are going to take it in turns to tell a bit of the story. It will be each person's turn when the 'teddy' is passed to them

- As you hold the 'teddy', make some suggestions about how the story could start, e.g. 'One windy morning' or 'Once upon a time' or 'It was a long, long time ago

157

when'. Or if your child or children are older, perhaps they can come up with their own favourite story starter

■ You then say whatever has been chosen, e.g. 'Once upon a time' and follow it with e.g. 'there was a tall, bright sunflower that was nodding gently in the morning breeze . . .'

■ Pass the 'teddy' to the next person. They then need to tell the next part of the story but using another object that is in front of you all, e.g. 'when he saw a sausage running by in a great hurry . . .'

■ The 'teddy' is then passed along, and the story continues. The sentences the children offer can be longer or shorter so long as they contain the object with the same initial sound

■ The game ends when all of the objects have been included in the story. The last person ends the story. Encourage the use of a great story ending such as 'and they all lived happily ever after!', or 'and that was how the story ended'

Additional ideas:

■ Older children might be able to repeat what has been said in the story so far, although that might be quite a challenge as there will be more and more to remember!

■ Perhaps they can think of additional objects that begin with the same sound to add to the story

■ If they are able, they could add descriptive words that start with the same sound as the objects e.g. the skinny sausage or the stripey sock!

Why?

The children will be challenged to really focus on what is being said in the story, to listen and remember. This will support the development of the executive function of working memory. The initial sound will reinforce their knowledge of those all-important sounds at the beginning of words.

Making other connections

Literacy connections will be made with the telling of the story, all good preparation for writing stories of their own, establishing an understanding of 'story starters', beginning-middle-endings and a rich story vocabulary is being supported.

Bottle Spies

This is a quiet and soothing activity that can be played anywhere.

What you'll need:

■ A clear, empty and dry bottle or bottles filled with rice or lentils and to which six small objects have been added. The objects might be keys, small world animals or insects, a sequin, a pen, a button, a conker, an acorn, a tiny spoon, a sweet, a leaf or twig, a ring . . . anything small enough to fit in the bottleneck and be hidden in the rice/lentils

Figure 8.3 A photograph of a Kilner jar full of lentils and small items.
Source: Photograph taken by the author

Step by step:

■ Show the bottle/s to your child or children. Allow them to hold the bottle, turn it and see that there are some things hidden inside

■ Tell them that there are six different things inside each bottle and challenge them to find them all or at least have a really good look to see what is inside their bottle

■ You could then introduce a game to them. Say that you are going to play 'I Spy' using the initial sounds of the things inside. You might say, 'I spy with my little eye, something beginning with "c"' (saying a soft 'cccc' sound without the schwar as in 'c-uh'. Be aware that this will be the sound for 'cat' or 'key' as we are just thinking of the sound [phoneme], not the letter [grapheme] at this stage)

■ Give the children time and support to find something. If you are playing with a group, they may not all have something beginning with all of the sounds in their bottles

■ Play again with a second sound and continue until all objects are found and/or the children remain focused

Additional ideas:

■ You could play the game again, but this time the children could find rhyming objects e.g. 'I spy . . . something that rhymes with SING', or 'MUTTON' depending on what you have hidden inside the bottles

Why?

This calm activity will help children become engrossed in searching for objects, really focusing on the initial sounds they are trying to match. They will need to hold the information in their head about the sound they are hunting for whilst they are actively looking.

Making other connections

Personal, Social and Emotional Development will be honed as the children focus on this quiet activity and they persevere to find the objects in the bottle. **Physical Development** will be supported as they sit, hold and manipulate the bottle in this activity.

Bedtime Treasure

This skill is a culmination of all the other activities – the skill of aurally blending sounds. This is a great calming bedtime activity or can, of course, be undertaken at any time of day!

What you'll need:

- An empty pillowcase

- A selection of objects from your child's bedroom that are really familiar to them

Figure 8.4 A photograph of a child in their bedroom holding a pillow case.
Source: Photograph taken by the author

Step by step:

- This game is good for children who are beginning to be able to blend sounds aurally e.g. when you say 'c-a-t', they can put those sounds together and say 'cat' independently

- Place the objects inside the pillowcase. If the game is new, this could be done with your child. They could help you to find the things to go into the pillowcase

■ You will then secretly look inside the pillowcase and 'sound out' an object e.g. 'b-oo-k' or 's-o-ck'. Some might be longer, such as 's-l-i-pp-er-s'

■ Your child has to guess what it might be from the sounds. When they guess correctly, take the objects out of the pillowcase

■ Once the objects are all out of the pillowcase, your child could replace them when you say an object's initial sound e.g. you say 'sss' and they put the slipper back, or you say a soft 'p' and they put the pyjamas back!

Additional ideas:

■ When your child is accustomed to playing the game, they could take your role and be the person to sound out the objects in the pillowcase

■ You could also secretly place the objects into the pillowcase, so your child doesn't have a clue what's inside!

Why?

All of our activities have been building up to this skill. Ensuring each child has the ability to hear individual sounds and then develop the skill to blend them together to read and pull them apart (segment) to spell. This will stand children in good stead for when they learn the letter shapes and sounds (graphemes and phonemes) and start to read and write independently.

Making other connections

Taking part in this activity will also develop skills in **Personal, Social and Emotional Development** and **Communication and Language** as you play together, take turns, promote listening and follow instructions. It will hone their **Literacy** skills in preparation for reading.

Syllable Shopping

This activity could take place when you are out shopping with your child or when working with children in a role play shop.

What you'll need:

- Up to four plastic shopping bags with labels on them – 1, 2, 3 and 'more'

Figure 8.5 A photograph of four large shopping bags numbered 1,2,3 and 'more' on a wooden floor.
Source: Photograph taken by the author

Step by step:

- When you are in the role play shop or out shopping with your child (or even at home!), gather together the numbered shopping bags and explain to your child that you are going to play a shopping game

- Ask your child to pass you/find a specific item from your shopping list e.g. 'porridge' or 'tom-a-toes', and clap as you say the word. Encourage your child to tell you how many claps the word had

■ Then, they need to find the correct bag that the object goes into. Explain that the claps are the number of 'syllables' the word has. *It is good for the child to hear the word 'syllables' although their understanding might be limited at this early stage. It is important for them to feel/clap the syllables as this will help their future reading*

■ Continue the game as you gather more items from your shop. Talk to your child about which bag has the most items in it when you are finished

Additional ideas:

■ You and your child or children could write the shopping list together. You can model writing the list as your child chooses what you will 'buy'

■ If your child is becoming competent at counting the syllables in the items, let them have a turn at sounding them out. They could ask you for the 'baked-beans' perhaps!

Why?

The understanding of syllables is important for future reading when children are learning the phonemes (letter sounds), matching them to graphemes (letter shapes) and blending them to read. It will support children when they come to read new words if they are familiar with syllables, as they will be more skilled at 'chunking' unfamiliar words into smaller parts to read them.

Making other connections

Understanding the World will be a great connection here if you are able to take your child or a group of children to a real shop for this activity. Learning about familiar processes and their local environment.

Water Skittles

A lovely physical game that could be played equally well both indoors and outside!

What you'll need:

- Five plastic bottles, partly filled with water, with a label on with a picture of an object that is familiar to your child or children e.g. bee, hat, rainbow, sunshine, dog, umbrella, hammer . . .

- A ball that is heavy enough for the children to knock over the bottles with but not too heavy for them to roll!

Figure 8.6 A photograph of a green bottle with an umbrella picture on it and a red ball on a table outside.
Source: Photograph taken by the author

Step by step:

- Find a suitable space for this game, either indoors or outside

- Place the labelled bottles in a row about two metres from where your child or children will be standing. They will need to roll the ball to knock the bottles over

165

- Talk about the pictures on the bottles with the children. Do they know what they all are?

- Explain that you are going to say a letter sound that one of the pictures begins with. Taking turns, the children will need to work out which one it is and then roll the ball to knock over the bottle. For example, you might say the sound 'u'. The first child will then attempt to knock over the bottle with the picture of the umbrella on it

- The children might find it a challenge to roll their balls accurately to knock over the bottles, so allow them to move closer if this is the case

- The game will finish when all of the bottles are knocked over. You can then stand the bottles up and play the game again!

Additional ideas:

- As the children become good at rolling the ball and knocking down the bottles, you could move them further back from the bottles to provide more challenge

- A competent child could take over the adult role in the game and call out the initial sounds. As the children start to match phonemes and graphemes, you could add the initial letters (graphemes) to the pictures

Why?

This game is a fun and lively way of encouraging children to hear the initial sounds in words, an important strategy for when they begin to read independently.

Making other connections

Clear links here to **Physical Development,** with the children being required to roll the ball accurately to knock over the bottles. The social aspect and turn-taking nature of the game will support elements of **Personal, Social and Emotional Development.**

Syllable Shimmy!

This is a fun activity that is full of movement to get the children really active!

What you'll need:

■ A selection of colourful 'pom poms' for the children to wave as they move. Alternatively, you could also use 'chiffon' type scarves or ribbons to wave

Figure 8.7 A photograph of some purple pom poms on a table outside.
Source: Photograph taken by the author

Step by step:

■ Gather your child or children in a suitably large space so they can move freely. This could be outdoors, in a performance space or even in a PE session if you are in a school

- Explain that you are going to shout out a word describing the way they need to move and the children need to move, shaking their pom-poms to the syllables in the words you say. For example, you might say 'sha-king', and the children need to shake their pom-poms twice in the air – one for each syllable, saying the word loudly as they move! This will clearly demonstrate to you their understanding of syllables

- Continue the game, calling out other words such as 'twist-ing', 'spinn-ing', 'turn-ing', 'pir-ou-et-ing' (a ballet spin!), 'stretch-ing' . . . or any others you can come up with! The children might be able to think of some words, too

Additional ideas:

- Challenge the children to make a dance pattern of the words in a sequence such as 'sha-king – spin-ing – wo-bl-ing'! Lots of energy will be used up in this game!

- To add a musical element, either you or another competent child or children could play a drum, tambourine or shake maracas at the same time. The children could even have maracas in one hand and a pom-pom in the other!

Why?

This is a lovely, lively way to engage children in internalising their understanding of syllables with the movements. As mentioned, it will also give you a good idea of who can and cannot understand syllables yet, therefore, giving you the opportunity to support them further with this learning.

Making other connections

Skills in **Physical Development** will be used as the children move in time to the syllables. **Expressive Arts and Design** could be another strong connection with the musical aspect of the 'additional idea'.

Circular Rhymes

In this activity, the children will develop some physical skills alongside listening to and making sounds.

What you'll need:

- A length of rope, ribbon, some lycra, an old scrunchy hose pipe – something long that children can hold in a circle. If there are a very small number of you, you could use a hula hoop

- A piece of ribbon

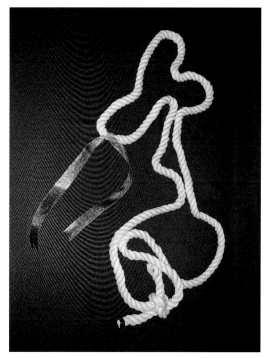

Figure 8.8 A photograph of a circle of rope with a golden ribbon tied to it.
Source: Photograph taken by the author

Step by step:

- **To enjoy playing this game, your child or children should know a number of nursery rhymes well**

- Sit or stand around your circle of material or hoop and encourage the children to hold it with both hands

■ Tie a piece of ribbon to the circle or hoop

■ Explain to the child or children that you are going to move the fabric/hoop around in a circle (show them in which direction it will travel) and that when the ribbon is dangling in front of the next person in the circle, they will say a line of a nursery rhyme

■ As the adult, you could start the game with the ribbon in front of you. You might say (or sing) 'Hey Diddle Diddle the cat and the fiddle . . .' and then stop

■ Move the circle around until the ribbon is in front of the next person, and they need to say or sing, 'The cow jumped over the moon'

■ The game then continues until the rhyme is finished! If anyone becomes stuck when it is their turn, then the rest of you can help them out

Additional ideas:

■ Invite the children to choose a nursery rhyme for you all to sing

■ When a child chooses a rhyme to sing, the game could start with them. Move the circle around until the ribbon is in front of them, then off you go!

■ You could enlist a 'conductor' with a musical instrument, some bells perhaps. You all keep passing the circle or hoop around until the instrument is played, and whoever has the ribbon in front of them takes their turn to say a line of the rhyme

Why?

This game will encourage the use and knowledge of a range of nursery rhymes, all picking out different rhyming words at the end of the lines of the song. Children will naturally tune into these rhymes, tuning into their similar sounds that will support their later phonic learning.

Making other connections

This activity will help develop skills in **Physical Development** if you use something heavier, such as a rope, for the children to pass around. This will develop their hand/upper body/arm/shoulder strength – all good preparation for holding a pencil and writing!

What Can You Tell Me?

Getting the most out of books (or pictures) without words!

What you'll need:

■ A good quality picture book/book without words (see www.therightstartearlyyears.co.uk) or a busy, interesting child-friendly picture. If you are able, gather a selection of these books or pictures, the child can choose which you will share

Figure 8.9 A photograph of a child with books.
Source: Photograph taken by the author

Step by step:

■ Sit with your child or children in a quiet place where you are both comfortable

■ Invite your/a child to choose a book for you to share

■ Ensure your child or children can see the pictures in the book

■ The first time you do this activity, just examine the pictures and talk about what you can see. Draw the child's attention to the book and ask them questions such as: 'What do you think is happening here?', 'Have you ever done that . . . ?' or 'I wonder why . . . is there?'.

■ Then, the next time, tell a story from the picture book. Just make one up from what you see or what you imagine might be happening

■ Start with 'Once upon a time' or 'One dark and stormy night . . .' depending on the picture on the page you are looking at. Encourage the child/ren to ask questions and make comments throughout

Additional ideas:

■ If the story is really enjoyed, you could scribe it (or make a recording of it). Write the story on a large piece of paper or in a homemade book. Say each word as you write, modelling writing in this way to your child/ren. If you tell a different story each time, you can write it down. This will help children to understand the importance of learning to write. Spoken words disappear, but once they are written, we can keep them forever!

Why?

This activity will encompass some of the very early elements of reading. It will encourage the child to engage with books, develop their vocabulary and make connections in their thinking. When they listen to you telling a story, they will absorb the language. Interestingly, even when a book has words, the children assume you are 'reading the picture'! Learning the language of stories from an early age is a gift that will support both their reading and writing in the future.

Making other connections

Quite clearly, there are strong connections with **Literacy Development** here, as mentioned in the preceding 'why?' box. The cosy warmth of sharing a book together will create a positive emotional environment for the child, securing elements of their **Personal, Social and Emotional Development. Expressive Arts and Design Development** will be supported as the children use their imaginations to help tell a story. This will stand them in good stead not only for writing their own stories but also when playing imaginative games such as in a Role Play space. Make-believe is such a valuable activity where children can explore so many elements of their lives safely and securely.

Voice Changers

This activity is great for having fun with your voice but will also establish skills for the activity 'Rhyme Voice Changers', which develops an awareness of voice sounds and is preparation for characterisations when children can read independently.

What you'll need:

■ A spinner or die with pictures of 'characters' on such as an ogre, a mouse, a fairy, an elephant, a bee and a cow, for example. You can add any you like

Figure 8.10 A photograph of a spinner with 'characters' on each section, such as an octopus, a donkey and a fairy.
Source: Photograph taken by the author

Step by step:

■ Sit with your child or group of children. This activity can be undertaken anywhere you are comfortable

- If you are using a spinner for the first time, allow the children time to practice spinning it effectively

- Explain that you are going to take turns to spin the spinner or roll the dice. Whichever picture it lands on is the voice the person whose turn it is needs to adopt when you ask them questions. You might ask, 'Hello, what is your name', or 'What did you have for breakfast today?'. You can ask any question you like, but the answer from the child whose turn it is needs to be in character. If it were the cow, they might answer 'My name is Bluebell' in a moo-ing kind of voice, or 'I had lots of lovely green grass for my breakfast' in a similar voice. You might need to model this first

- Take turns to spin the spinner or roll the dice. The adult needs to ask the questions, but everyone can enjoy the answers! If you are playing with one child, see the 'additional ideas'

Additional ideas:

- When the children become good at playing the game and answering the questions, they can then become the questioner

- If you are playing the game with one child, you could create some question cards if they might find it hard to think of their own questions. This will then enable you to take turns effectively

Why?

This will teach children how they can change their voices and also encourage them to listen to the voice changes of others. This will help them tune into sounds which will eventually support them in their later phonics learning.

Making other connections

Literacy skills will be supported, as mentioned previously. When the children are reading confidently and independently, it is important that they are able to read with expression and fluency. Tuning into characterisations in this way will build this experience for them. **Personal, Social and Emotional Development** will again be supported by the turn-taking aspect of this game. The fun and laughter it will invoke will support wellbeing!

Tap and Sing

Confidence and a broadening vocabulary are established as children learn and can join in with Nursery Rhymes and other favourite songs

What you'll need:

- A selection of 'beaters' that are safe to tap with

- A small selection of 'drums' to create your own drum kit e.g. a plastic bucket, a cardboard box, a saucepan, a plastic food container or bottle, an old tyre, a wooden container or a large glass (milk-type) bottle (with appropriate supervision)

Figure 8.11 A photograph of a cake tin, a metal colander, some small metal bowls and a wooden spoon.
Source: Photograph taken by the author

Step by step:

- Find a space to sit with your child/ren and place the drum-kit items and 'beaters' in front of you

175

- Ask your child to pick their favourite 'beater' and explore the 'drum-kit', tapping each and listening to the sound. Then move two 'drums' to one side

- Model how to tap a steady beat on one 'drum' as you start to sing a song or nursery rhyme e.g. 'One, two, three, four, five. Once I caught a fish alive . . .' and encourage your child to join in

- Sing again, perhaps the same song, but this time add another 'drum' and tap the two different 'drums' as you sing

- Then, sing the song again, adding the third 'drum' to create a 'drum-kit', modelling how to use all three as you sing. Invite your child to choose another song to sing and continue to play!

Additional ideas:

- You could change your beater or use two beaters

- Try keeping the steady beat, although small children are often very happy to tap the syllables to the song they are singing

Why?

Singing a broad range of nursery rhymes tunes children into rhyme as a strategy to support early reading as well as broadens their vocabulary as they learn new words. Tapping along to the song internalises the rhythm, which engages the child with the pulse or metre of the rhyme. Tapping syllables supports their understanding of how words work prior to them learning to read.

Making other connections

Clear links here to **Expressive Arts and Design** with music and learning to play a 'drum'. **Physical Development** skills will be honed with playing the drums and the co-ordination needed to play a steady pulse or tap the syllables!

Singing Scarves

This activity will get children's brains working as they sing a song and engage in physical activity at the same time!

What you'll need:

■ A selection of colourful 'chiffon' type floaty scarves (select a size of scarf that is appropriate for the children you are working with)

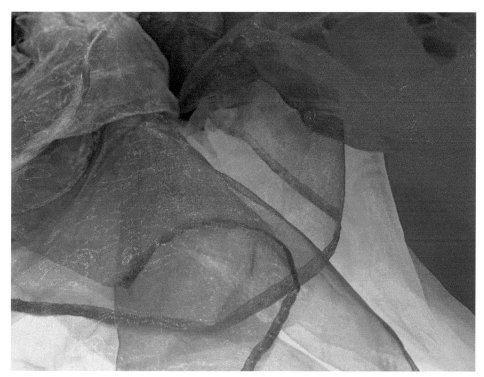

Figure 8.12 A photograph of a collection of coloured chiffon scarves.
Source: Photograph taken by the author

Step by step:

■ Gather the children together and show them the selection of scarves. Invite them to choose one, perhaps one that is their favourite colour

■ Explore the scarves a little and ask questions about how they feel. Are they heavy? Encourage the children to move them, then show them how to throw them up into the air and then catch them

■ Ask the children to hold their scarves still and explain that you are going to sing a nursery rhyme as you throw your scarf up in the air. You are going to sing the rhyme, but only until you catch the scarf on its way down! Then you will stop singing. Invite the children to help you to choose a song to sing, e.g. 'Humpty Dumpty . . .'

■ You need to model how to do this to the children. Tell the children that you will show them first. As you start to sing, throw the scarf as high in the air as you can. As soon as you catch it, stop singing. Talk to the children about which word you were on when you had to stop singing e.g. 'had'!

■ If you have one child or a small group, let the child or one of the children have a turn. All sing together to see which word you end on. You could model writing the word beside the child's name so you don't forget. Take turns and see who gets furthest through the song

■ Keep taking turns to see if you can improve your 'score'

Additional ideas:

■ Choose a different nursery rhyme to sing and throw your scarves to

■ Talk about the speed of the song. If they sing faster, do they get to a different place in the song?

Why?

This will be a different way of engaging your child or children with nursery rhymes to embed them in their early learning. Discussing which word they get to will focus on the words in the song and realising that if they sing faster, they will get further, too!

Making other connections

Some skills in **Physical Development** will be honed – eye-hand co-ordination is a priority to ensure the scarf is caught whilst the child is engaged in singing at the same time! **Literacy** will be highlighted with the singing of songs and the discussion about the words and the modelling of writing.

Shopping List Game

This is a great game to encourage children to really listen and hold information in their heads, too – a great executive function!

What you'll need:

■ A small, child-sized shopping basket

■ Some real shopping items e.g. a loaf of bread, an orange, a banana, some washing-up liquid, a milk bottle, some biscuits, a tin of baked beans, some cheese, some onions, etc.

Figure 8.13 A photograph of some shopping – two tins, a packet of crisps and some biscuits on a tray with a plant.
Source: Photograph taken by the author

Step by step:

■ Sit with your child or invite a small group of children to sit in a circle on the floor. If your children are younger, place the shopping items in the space in front of you/ them, talk through naming them and ask if the children have ever seen them before/ eaten them, etc.

■ Explain that the children are going to help you make up a shopping list, but as you have no pencil or paper, you are all going to have to remember the shopping list as well as you can!

■ Tell the children that you will pass the shopping bag around the circle, and when each child holds the bag, they will say an item that they would like to buy from the selection in front of them saying, 'I am going to buy a . . .'. They then pass the bag to the next person, who will say the previous person's item and add their own, e.g. 'I will buy a banana and an onion'. The game continues with the children adding to the list as they go. The game stops when a person cannot remember all of the things that went in the basket before.

Additional ideas:

■ There are various ways to adapt this game, as it can be quite challenging! To start with, the children could place the items in the bag as they say them. These can then be referred to by the next person. The thing they will have to remember is the order in which they went in! They could then move to playing more of a memory game without placing the items in the bag

■ You could remove all of the props for older children, and they could generate their own ideas for items

■ The game could be tailored to any particular theme your children are currently interested in. You could be park keepers gathering up autumnal items, or you could be packing a suitcase for a holiday!

Why?

This is a game that requires children to really listen to what has been said and to focus and concentrate on what others are saying. It is quite a challenge, and small children will not be able to remember many items – or they may surprise you! As mentioned, this is perfect for supporting working memory, the mental process of holding information in your head.

Making other connections

Personal, Social and Emotional skills will be developed through the turn-taking nature of this game, and the children may well support each other with memorising the shopping lists. If you add the additional ideas, then **Understanding the World** will be another connection in a variety of ways depending on the category of items you are gathering.

Rhyme Voice Changers

This activity builds on the skills honed in Voice Changers but adds a rhyming element.

What you'll need:

- A spinner or die with pictures of 'characters' on such as an ogre, a mouse, a fairy, an elephant, a bee, a witch/wizard, a snake or a cow, for example. You can add any you like

- A spinner or die with pictures or words depicting nursery rhymes e.g. 'Humpty Dumpty,' 'Hey Diddle Diddle' or 'One, Two, Three, Four, Five. Once I caught a fish alive' (see 'additional ideas' for further information)

Figure 8.14 A photograph with two dice with pictures of characters and pictures depicting nursery rhymes.
Source: Photograph taken by the author

Step by step:

- Sit with your child or group of children. This activity can be undertaken anywhere you are comfortable

- If you are using a spinner for the first time, allow the children time to practice spinning it effectively

- Explain that you are going to take turns to spin the spinner or roll the dice. Whichever picture it lands on is the voice the turn-taker needs to adopt

- The first player spins that spinner (or rolls the dice)

- Then, they need to spin the nursery rhyme spinner (or roll the dice) to select a rhyme

- Once this has been done, encourage the child to sing or recite the rhyme in the voice of the character they previously selected. For example, they sing 'Humpty Dumpty' in the voice of a mouse!

- It is then the turn of the next player. Keep playing for as long as the children are focused and enjoying the game

Additional ideas:

- If you have wooden spoons with nursery rhyme pictures on them or nursery rhyme cards, these could be used instead of the second spinner or dice. They could be hidden in a drawstring bag and selected by the player when it's their turn

- To extend the game further, you could add the dice from the Fast and Slow game; then the nursery rhyme also has to be sung at the speed rolled on the dice!

Why?

This game will establish the control children have over their voices further still and encourage them to tune into sounds. It will also further embed, remind and reinforce the all-important nursery rhymes.

Making other connections

Literacy, as with Voice Changers, the characterisations will support later reading skills as well as supporting the children to tune into sound. As with Voice Changers again, **Personal, Social and Emotional Development** will be supported, with the turn-taking aspect of this game. The fun and laughter it will invoke will support wellbeing!

Alliteration Launch

This activity can be undertaken outdoors or just as well inside!

What you'll need:

- A dice with some pictures stuck or drawn on it – or a spinner with pictures on it (see Figure 8.15)

- A selection of balls or bean bags

- A selection of buckets with pictures on them that start with the same sound as those on the dice or spinner e.g. hat/hand, dog/dinner, pig/pencil, bag/belt, mountain/mat, cup/carrot, foot/fairy, leg/light, sun/seesaw, apple/ant . . .

Figure 8.15 A photograph of four beanbags, a die and two labelled buckets on grass.
Source: Photograph taken by the author

Step by step:

- Invite your child or children to sit together in a large space either indoors or outside

- Explain the rules of the game to them. They will take turns to roll the dice or spin the spinner. They will then pick up a small ball or bean bag. They will then say the word that is face-up on the dice or at the bottom of the spinner

Sounds With Words

- They will look at the buckets and decide which of the pictures on the bucket starts with the same sound as the one on their die/spinner

- Invite the child to stand a short distance from the buckets and try to throw the ball/ bean bag into the correct bucket i.e. the one that has a picture that starts with the same sound as they have on their die/spinner. Always allow them several attempts if they are unsuccessful!

- It is then the next person's turn to roll the die/spin the spinner, and the game continues until all of the balls have been used up. It doesn't matter if the same picture is rolled or spun. The child can still say the rhyme. You can always make the game last longer by emptying the buckets and re-using the balls!

Additional ideas:

- You could extend the activity by encouraging the children to invent nonsense alliterative strings from the words. The alliterative words can be real or made up e.g. bag-bun-bounce-brolly-band-butterfly-biscuit-bread-baddie-bumpy . . . you could count how many words each child gets in their string to see who's was the longest!

Why?

Understanding alliteration will tune a child's ear into those all-important initial sounds that will help them when they blend aurally and then blend sounds to read independently.

Making other connections

As with the Rhyme launch game, **Personal, Social and Emotional Development** will be enhanced through the social nature of this game, taking turns and waiting patiently for their turn. Thinking of rhymes will support **Literacy** and, of course, there is the added **Physical Development** skill of throwing the balls or bean bags accurately into the buckets!

Rhyme Time Stop!

Here, you will ensure children really know their Nursery Rhymes well! The activity will demonstrate both their understanding of rhyme and how well they are able to listen and focus on language.

What you'll need:

- A range of nursery rhymes that you both/all know well (see appendix or www. therightstartearlyyears.co.uk)

Figure 8.16 A photograph of a child laughing, holding a hand up to indicate stop.
Source: Photograph taken by the author

Step by step:

- Sit with your child or group of children. This activity can be undertaken absolutely anywhere!

Sounds With Words

- You will need to ensure that you have previously taught the child/ren the nursery rhymes you are going to use in this game. Singing them regularly to embed the words

- Make sure the children are focusing on you and say you are going to sing to them, and they need to listen carefully. Choose one of the rhymes they know and start to sing it, but miss out a significant word

- Start by missing out the last word in a line e.g. Humpty Dumpty sat on a . . ., Humpty Dumpty had a great . . .

- Encourage the children to fill in the missing word for you – they may well do this without prompting!

- When they are accomplished at doing this, move to omitting less significant word e.g. Humpty Dumpty had a . . . fall

- Undoubtedly, the children will roar with laughter at how silly you are to miss out a word and will be thrilled to help you put your mistake right

Additional ideas:

- Invite the children to take turns choosing the nursery rhyme for you to sing

- See if your child/ren can be the singer in the game and miss out a word! This is quite a challenge!

Why?

This activity is another way to engage the children in the singing of nursery rhymes. The first part of the activity will focus very particularly on the missing rhyming words, making that connection even firmer in their minds.

Making other connections

Singing will clearly involve **Expressive Arts and Design** skills. **Literacy** skills will be developed both as the children focus on and add in the rhyming words and also with the second part of the activity, focusing on the other vocabulary in the songs. The focused listening that is required will also support this element of **Literacy.**

Rhyme Launch

This activity can be undertaken outdoors or just as well inside!

What you'll need:

- A die with some pictures stuck or drawn on it – or a spinner with pictures on it

- A selection of balls or bean bags

- A selection of buckets with pictures on that rhyme with those on the die or spinner e.g. boat/goat, hen/pen, bat/cat, rat/mat, tap/cap, dog/log, bed/head, pin/tin, van/pan, zig-zag/bag

Figure 8.17 A photograph of two buckets with pictures on, a wooden die and four coloured beanbags.
Source: Photograph taken by the author

Step by step:

- Gather your children or child and sit together in a large space either indoors or outside

- Explain that they will take turns to roll the die or spin the spinner. They will then pick up a small ball or bean bag

■ Invite the child to say the word that is face-up on the die or at the bottom of the spinner

■ Ask them to look at the buckets and decide which of the pictures on the bucket rhymes with the word on the die/spinner

■ They then have to stand a distance from the bucket and try to throw the ball/bean bag into the rhyming bucket. Allow them a few attempts if they are unsuccessful!

■ It is then the next person's turn to roll the die/spin the spinner, and the game continues until all of the balls have been used up. It doesn't matter if the same picture is rolled or spun. The child can still say the rhyme. You can always make the game last longer by emptying the buckets and re-using the balls!

Additional ideas:

■ You could extend the activity by encouraging the children to invent nonsense rhyming strings from the words. The rhyming words can be real or made up e.g. hen-pen-fen-men-len-zen-ten-when-bren . . . you could count how many words each child gets in their string to see whose was the longest!

Why?

Young children sometimes find it quite hard to hear rhymes, which are an important strategy to master to support early reading. Playing a lot of games such as these will help those children embed this skill.

Making other connections

Personal, Social and Emotional Development will be enhanced through the social nature of this game, taking turns and waiting patiently for their turn. Thinking of rhymes will support **Literacy** and, of course, there is the added **Physical Development** skill of throwing the balls or bean bags accurately into the buckets!

Nature Hunt

Here you will be focusing on initial sounds in words whilst having fun outside!

What you'll need:

- A muffin (baking) tray, an empty egg box or a tens frame

- Small containers in which each child can place their gathered objects

- Small pieces of paper and/or a marker pen for writing initial letters

- An outdoor space – *check for safety before undertaking this activity, not forgetting plants that might be dangerous and/or sharp or dangerous objects*

Figure 8.18 A photograph of autumnal leaves, small gourds, sweet chestnut cases, acorns, conkers, a flower and a tens frame on hessian.
Source: Photograph taken by the author

Step by step:

- Gather your children or child and sit together outside

- Write letters on your pieces of paper, say them as you write and place one in each section of your tray, box or frame

- *If your child is not at the stage of recognising letters, draw pictures of objects that start with the same initial sound as the things you expect your child to find – e.g. flag to match with flower,*

189

sun to match with *stick* – and support them by emphasising the initial sound when they place the objects in the tray

■ Explain that they are going to go on a treasure hunt outdoors to look for things that start with the sounds that are in your tray

■ The child or children run around finding all manner of things to place in the tray – they will need to be aware of the size of the things they find! You can support this part of the activity by talking to the children as they forage

■ Bring your children back together and gather around the tray, box, frame/s and talk as the children place their objects in the correct places

Additional ideas:

■ You could make up a silly story from the objects you have all gathered

■ See if the children can think of rhyming words to go with the objects they have found e.g. leaf/thief, stone/moan, mud/flood . . .

■ Don't forget to draw the children's attention to sounds they can hear when outside, too!

Why?

Some children respond differently to learning when it is taken outdoors and become more engaged, animated and better able to focus on any task. It is important that you respond to all children's individual learning preferences. The children will make strong connections with initial sounds, good preparation for learning to read and the additional activities will encompass other important areas such as rhyme.

Making other connections

Physical Development will be supported by the movement and outdoor activity. **Communication and Language** will be supported by the children engaging in conversation about the things they are finding and where they will be placed in the box or frame. Whichever container you use, a **Mathematics** element will be present with one object being placed in one space. If you use a tens frame, then the additional maths content will be greater! How many have we got so far, how many more are needed . . . ?

Musical Medley

As mentioned in the book, if you are able to play just three chords on a guitar, it will make this a Magical Musical Medley!

What you'll need:

■ A guitar and the confidence to play just the chords D, A7 and C

■ Your voice and a plethora of Nursery Rhymes that you know by heart

Figure 8.19 A photograph of an adult playing a guitar with a small child watching.
Source: Photograph taken by the author

Step by step:

■ Find a space to sit with your child or children and invite them to sing with you

■ Start strumming your guitar as an introduction, or just start to sing

■ For this singing activity, just let the children join in with you as and when they can. They will thoroughly enjoy moving from rhyme to rhyme and get excited about the ones they know best!

■ You just keep singing, going from song to song, without a break. The order can be any that you like, keeping the pitch the same. You could sing the following:

Mary Mary Quite Contrary
Twinkle Twinkle Little Star

191

Fee Fi Fiddly I O
Humpty Dumpty Sat on a Wall
Three Blind Mice
Hickory Dickory Dock
Baa Baa Black Sheep
Goosey Goosey Gander
Eensy Weensy Spider
Little Bo Peep
Jack and Jill

■ The fun of it all is to just keep going without stopping!

Additional ideas:

■ You could encourage the children to tap or clap along with the rhythm, or when they are accustomed to the activity, introduce some musical instruments!

■ Have a selection of nursery rhyme prompt cards or spoons handy. The children could lay them out in a line, and you could sing along in that order, from left to right. The children could then access this activity independently during their play – with or without instruments

Why?

Children will sing joyfully, taking pride in the quantity of songs they know and can join in with. The rhymes and vocabulary will become embedded, and they can so easily access this activity independently with the suggestion in the 'additional ideas'.

Making other connections

Links can be made to **Expressive Arts and Design** with music and singing along to the guitar if possible. **Physical Development** skills will be honed with the playing of the instruments and can be supported and explored further during their independent play.

Missing Word

This activity builds listening skills with nursery rhyme knowledge.

What you'll need:

■ A soft toy or fun item to pass around a circle or between you and a child

Figure 8.20 A photograph of some wooden spoons with pictures on in a pot, felt pens and paper.
Source: Photograph taken by the author

Step by step:

■ Sit with your child or group of children. This activity can be undertaken anywhere you are comfortable

■ Explain that you are going to sing a song together and tell the children which song it is e.g. 'Pease Pudding hot, Pease Pudding cold . . .' and that as you sing, you are going to pass the soft toy from person to person (as in Pass the Parcel!). The passing of the toy can be practiced to ensure the children understand how to do this

Sounds With Words

- Now tell the child/ren that you are going to miss out a word, but they are not to tell you until the end of the song. The person who is holding the teddy at the end of the song is the one who tells you the missing word!

- Have a practice at playing the game without passing the soft toy around to ensure the children understand

- If it is just two of you playing the game and you end up holding the soft toy at the end of the song, pass it back to the child for them to give you the answer. Only the person holding the soft toy is allowed to give the answer!

- If they are right, celebrate! If they are not, you could sing the song again to try for a second time or they can choose who to give the soft toy to so that they can try to answer. Whichever will suit the children so they feel supported

- Play the game again with a different song

Additional ideas:

- You could have a die with nursery rhymes depicted on it, a spinner or wooden nursery rhyme spoons to choose the song or invite the children to choose a song

- If the children become accomplished at this game, they could take a turn to be the singer and try missing out a word. Not as easy as it sounds!

Why?

This game will require the children to listen really carefully to the words that are being sung to work out what the missing word is. This will ensure their listening is very focused.

Making other connections

Personal, Social and Emotional Development will be supported by this activity. The children will need to contain their enthusiasm to not call out the answer, which will help elements of self-regulation. **Literacy** and the use of rhyme and a broad vocabulary will be developed through the songs chosen to sing.

Fast and Slow

This activity will be fun and engaging whilst recalling an abundance of nursery rhymes!

What you'll need:

- A die with pictures depicting nursery rhymes drawn on each face
- A second die with fast written on three faces and slow written on the other three.

Figure 8.21 A photograph of two wooden dice with words on and depictions of nursery rhymes beside a cushion.
Source: Photograph taken by the author

Step by step:

- Sit with your child or encourage a small group of children to sit in a small circle
- Place the two dice on the floor and explain that the pictures depict nursery rhymes. See if the children can guess the rhymes and then check that they know them all. Practice singing them if needed.

- Then look at the second die and explain the words fast and slow

- Explain that the children will take turns to roll both dice. They will then sing the nursery rhyme that is facing upwards on the die at the speed depicted on the second die e.g. 'Baa Baa Black Sheep' sung slowly. This can be done individually or with all of you as a group, depending on confidence

Additional ideas:

- You could put animals or characters on the second die so the children sing in the manner of the character on the upward face of the die, such as a mouse (sing like a mouse!), an elephant, a shark or a giant!

- You could add other speeds or instructions to the second dice, such as high, low, whispering, shouting

Why?

It is a good skill for the children to recognise the sound changes and how to recreate them for themselves. They will demonstrate a developing understanding of loud and soft, for example. It will also develop early recognition of characterisation in preparation for when they are reading out loud as their reading competence grows and reading with expression.

Making other connections

Early **Literacy** skills are developed with the recognition of changes to voices and the recall of rhymes, an all-important early reading skill. Tuning into rhyme will support later phonic learning. **Expressive Arts and Design** will be supported with the singing and characterisations if you use the additional idea for the second die.

Book Sounds

This activity will encourage early reading and engagement with books.

What you'll need:

- A selection of books with no words (picture books). Alternatively, you could use a child-friendly picture or painting instead

Figure 8.22 A photograph of an adult and child looking at a picture.
Source: Photograph taken by the author

Step by step:

- Sit with your child or a group of children. Ensure all children can easily see the book or picture

- The adult can point to an object in the picture and ask a pondering question e.g. pointing to a waterfall, 'I wonder what this might sound like?'

- Model making that sound, perhaps 'swooooooosh' or 'whooooooosh', and encourage the child/children to join in

- Point to other objects, maybe a tree 'sssssshhhhhhhh', a bird 'fwup fwup' or 'cheep cheep', a bus 'nnnnnnmmmmmmm' then make the sound of the doors opening or the windscreen wipers!

- Encourage your child or children to identify objects in the pictures and invent sounds for them

Additional ideas:

- To remember the sounds or to share them with others, make a recording of each sound

- The recording could be used when the child is 'reading' the book alone later or to share it with another child

- Use the recording to try and make different sounds next time you share the book or picture

Why?

Early engagement with books is an essential part of learning to read. If the children can feel they are part of the 'reading', they will feel they are making a valuable contribution and will see themselves as a reader! Research has suggested that children really believe we are 'reading the pictures' when they are at this early stage of reading themselves.

Making other connections

As with many of our activities, skills in **Personal, Social and Emotional Development** will be honed through the sharing of a book. **Communication and Language** will also be supported through the discussion and the adult providing what might be new language as well as adding to the child's cultural awareness, an awareness of their own environment and that of others. Depending on the book or picture you choose, their **Understanding of the World** will also be heightened.

Ask Me a Question

Children turn the tables on you and ask you questions about a book or picture!

What you'll need:

■ Either a selection of books without words or a busy, child-friendly picture

Figure 8.23 A photograph of a child holding a book.
Source: Photograph taken by the author

Step by step:

■ Sit in a comfortable space with your child or children

■ Allow the children to choose the book or picture that you are going to look at. It will be best if you have previously modelled asking them questions whilst looking at books so that they understand their role in this activity

Sounds With Words

- Tell the children that today they are in charge and can ask you anything they would like to about the pictures in the book

- Encourage them to ask you questions and answer them fully, introducing new vocabulary if you are able. Answer in full sentences but make it conversational e.g. 'What a good question'. . . or 'I'd never thought of that, what a good question that is!'

- If they would like, encourage them to tell a story from the pictures if you have already modelled this previously. If not, take this opportunity to tell a story from the pictures to bring the activity to an end

Additional ideas:

- You could model writing to your child or children by making 'A Big Book of Questions'. When the child asks a question, write it down, explaining that then you will both/all remember it for next time. This book could then be used just for book-sharing occasions or you could use it more widely for all sorts of wonderful questions that you could ask other people!

Why?

Listening to a story without using pictures or books to support the telling is a great skill for children to learn. It will help to develop their listening skills and also encourage them to use their imaginations – visualising the pictures in their minds!

Making other connections

There are strong connections with **Literacy Development** here, in the children being able to listen to a story, visualise events and eventually retell the story for themselves. Also beneficial is the story being scribed, modelling writing and the children making their own marks, too. **Communication and Language** is well-supported, with the child being required to ask the questions. **Expressive Arts and Design** development will occur with the musical skill of adding a soundtrack to the story. An **IT** element could easily be added if you record or video the story to listen to or share with others later.

Animal Tongue Twisters

This activity has so many opportunities for playing it anywhere! It is the alliteration that is the important part of the activity.

What you'll need:

- Your voices

Figure 8.24 A photograph of two small world characters, some farm animals, a small house, a plant pot and green chiffon on grass.
Source: Photograph taken by the author

Step by step:

- Join your child as they play, share a story or take this activity to a child and engage them in play. *This activity could be undertaken when you are sharing a book together or when playing with small world toys. It could also be created as an activity that you take to a child in a small world basket or box. Play together and invent tongue twisters*

- Identify an animal, such as a 'hen'. Say the word 'hen' once or twice as if pondering, then add a descriptive word before 'hen' such as 'hungry hen' or 'happy hen', or perhaps 'hairy horse'

Sounds With Words

- Encourage your child to repeat the phrase after you and then see if they can come up with their own ideas

Additional ideas:

- You could provide challenge by adding more words to the phrase, for example 'Molly the muddy monkey'

- See if your child can come up with more lengthy alliterative phrases. You could make a book of tongue twisters to share with others!

- Teach your child some other well-known alliterative tongue twisters such as 'Round and round the rugged rock the ragged rascal ran'

Why?

Alliteration will help the children to really listen to the initial sounds in words, tuning their ears into sounds that are the same in preparation for phonic learning. It is an enjoyable activity with familiar objects, making listening to sounds fun and extending their vocabulary!

Making other connections

Literacy connections are clear with alliteration, and **Personal, Social and Emotional Development** can be developed in having fun with another person, supporting the making of relationships. It is hard to say some of the tongue twisters, so **Communication and Language,** speaking in particular, with grouping words by their initial sound.

Appendix

Planning tool – potential 'Early Phonics' opportunities for specific learners

Learning space	Resources	'Early phonics' possibilities	Initials of child/ren	Progress notes/ what to provide next
e.g. mark-making space	Three Nursery rhyme spoons	Add nursery rhyme spoons to reinforce knowledge of them – Twinkle Twinkle, Baa Baa Black Sheep, Humpty Dumpty	Children for whom these skills are important to develop **RB**	RB accessed these twice this week and made a small picture book of them. Change to three different spoons to broaden experience

Planning tool – potential 'Early Phonics' opportunities in a learning environment

Learning space	Resources	'Early phonics' possibilities Conversation starters, thoughts, ideas drawing attention to sounds	Learning space	Resources	'Early phonics' possibilities Conversation starters, thoughts, ideas drawing attention to sounds
e.g. mark-making space	Pens – various; Pencils – variety fat/thin; Paper; card; sticky tape, masking tape, stapler; hole punch, split pins, scissors	**Draw the children's attention to:** Snapping scissors, sounds of scissors cutting, sounds different scissors make, sound of stapler, tearing/cutting paper, split pins tinkling . . . Sing or hum as you draw or write alongside the children **Conversation example . . .** 'I love the sound of that paper tearing! Do you? Does it remind you of anything? It makes me think of an aeroplane soaring through the sky!'			

Index